Mark Twain's Adventures of
Huckleberry Finn

DATE DUE			

Mark Twain's
ADVENTURES
OF
HUCKLEBERRY
FINN

Bloom's
NOTES

Edited and with an Introduction by
HAROLD BLOOM

Printed and bound in the United States of America.

First Printing
1 3 5 7 9 8 6 4 2

ISBN: 0-7910-3678-2

Chelsea House Publishers
1974 Sproul Road, Suite 400
P.O. Box 914
Broomall, PA 19008-0914

chelsea 7/99
15.26

Contents

User's Guide

This volume is designed to present biographical, critical, and bibliographical information on Mark Twain and *Adventures of Huckleberry Finn*. Following Harold Bloom's introduction, there appears a detailed biography of the author, discussing the major events in his life and his important literary works. Then follows a thematic and structural analysis of the work, in which significant themes, patterns, and motifs are traced. An annotated list of characters supplies brief information on the chief characters in the work.

A selection of critical extracts, derived from previously published material by leading critics, then follows. The extracts consist of statements by the author on his work, early reviews of the work, and later evaluations down to the present day. The items are arranged chronologically by date of first publication. A bibliography of Twain's writings (including a complete listing of all books he wrote, cowrote, edited, and translated in his lifetime, and important posthumous publications), a list of additional books and articles on him and on *Adventures of Huckleberry Finn,* and an index of themes conclude the volume.

Harold Bloom is Sterling Professor of the Humanities at Yale University and Henry W. and Albert A. Berg Professor of English at the New York University Graduate School. He is the author of twenty books and the editor of more than thirty anthologies of literature and literary criticism.

Professor Bloom's works include *Shelley's Mythmaking* (1959), *The Visionary Company* (1961), *Blake's Apocalypse* (1963), *Yeats* (1970), *A Map of Misreading* (1975), *Kabbalah and Criticism* (1975), and *Agon: Towards a Theory of Revisionism* (1982). *The Anxiety of Influence* (1973) sets forth Professor Bloom's provocative theory of the literary relationships between the great writers and their predecessors. His most recent books are *The American Religion* (1992) and *The Western Canon* (1994).

Professor Bloom earned his Ph.D. from Yale University in 1955 and has served on the Yale faculty since then. He is a 1985 MacArthur Foundation Award recipient and served as the Charles Eliot Norton Professor of Poetry at Harvard University in 1987–88. He is currently the editor of the Chelsea House series Major Literary Characters and Modern Critical Views, and other Chelsea House series in literary criticism.

Introduction

HAROLD BLOOM

For a country obsessed with the image of freedom, Huck Finn is an inevitable hero, since he incarnates the genius of American solitude. Richard Poirier observes that *Adventures of Huckleberry Finn* is marked by the quietness of its autobiographical narrator. Huck talks to us, the readers, but only rarely to the other figures in the book, even to his companion, Jim. Loneliness is the condition of Huck's existence; he belongs neither to the adult world, nor to that world's antechamber in Tom Sawyer's gang. Truly, Huck is as isolated and eccentric a figure as "Walt Whitman," the hero of *Song of Myself,* and Mark Twain, as Poirier remarks, never found a fit context for Huck after the first sixteen chapters of *Adventures.* Partly, this may mean that Huck is larger and more vital than his book, admirable as it is. But I suspect that ultimately Huck stands for what is least sociable in Mark Twain, whose discomfort with American culture was profound. Like Huck, Twain had decided to go to hell, if that was the only way to escape his neighbors and country, and if that was the only path to freedom.

Since Huck is neither a god nor a beast, he suffers intensely from his loneliness. If you define freedom as a relationship within society, then Huck is a negative image only: the hero as misfit. Classic American literature, however, does not easily permit societal definitions of freedom. Hester Prynne in *The Scarlet Letter,* Ishmael in *Moby-Dick,* Thoreau at Walden Pond, Emerson confronting the past: all provide images of isolation as an inner freedom, and the exiles of Henry James have a way of reestablishing their American solitude in centers of sociability like London and Rome. Whitman proclaims the love of brothers while finding his particular metaphor for poetic creativity in Onanism, and Emily Dickinson's self-segregation is notorious. The tradition does not vary that much in the great writers of our century, where our poets remain lonely: Robert Frost, Wallace Stevens, T. S. Eliot, Hart Crane, Elizabeth Bishop, John Ashbery. One thinks of the protagonists of our major novelists: Dreiser's Carrie, Cather's Ántonia, Fitzgerald's Gatsby, Faulkner's Joe

Christmas: these also are isolated dreamers. The American religion of self-reliance carries with it the burden that no American feels wholly free until she is truly alone.

Fitzgerald, Hemingway, and Faulkner all exalted *Adventures of Huckleberry Finn*, seeing in it their American starting point. Their tributes were rather fierce: Fitzgerald said that Huck's "eyes were the first eyes that ever looked at us objectively that were not eyes from overseas," while Hemingway placed the book first among all our books, and Faulkner's final novel, *The Rievers*, explicitly presents itself as a revision of Twain's masterpiece. What disconcerts many critics of *Huckleberry Finn*—the slippage between Huck as narrator, lying his way to a kind of freedom, and Huck as active character, ultimately manifesting a generosity of spirit beyond everyone else in the book except Jim—seems not to have bothered Twain's novelist descendants. Twain gave them a fascinating fourteen-year-old quasi-scoundrel in Huck, a trickster as resourceful as Homer's Odysseus or the biblical Jacob. Though Huck may look like an unvarying picaresque hero, he actually is a master of disguises, and he changes incessantly, while growing no older. He is very hard to characterize because he is not still long enough for us to know exactly who he is. Nor is his own sense of identity securely established: he both is and is not his dreadful father's son.

Huck's central freedom is essentially authentic: he always will be fourteen years old, because we cannot envision him, say, at forty. Lighting out for the territory will not age him; whether his morally ambiguous attitude toward society could survive maturation is therefore an inappropriate question. That may be why *Adventures of Huckleberry Finn* ends in a fashion unsatisfactory to nearly every critical reader the book has attracted. We all want Huck to be better and stronger, and even more self-reliant than he is. He has broken with the morality of slaveholding, but the break has ravaged and confused him. We cannot have a politically correct Huck, which is why the book continues to offend so many, who simply do not know enough nineteenth-century American history to see that—for his time, in his place—Huck is a miracle of self-emancipation. Yet he is not only pursued by the murderous Pap Finn; he also carries much

6

of his father within him, as Harold Beaver has shown. *Adventures of Huckleberry Finn* has only a few rivals as the indispensable work of nineteenth-century American literature: *Moby-Dick, Leaves of Grass, The Scarlet Letter* are among them. Ahab, "Walt Whitman," Hester Prynne all inform our sense of ourselves, but it is primarily in Huck Finn that we study our nostalgias. ✤

Biography of Mark Twain

Samuel Langhorne Clemens, who wrote under the pseudonym "Mark Twain," was born in Florida, Missouri, on November 30, 1835; he grew up mostly in Hannibal, Missouri, a town on the Mississippi River where he received only irregular schooling. Following his father's death in 1847 he was apprenticed to a printer and wrote for his brother's newspaper. From 1857 to 1861 he was a steamboat pilot on the Mississippi, and from 1862 he worked as a journalist in Nevada and California, adopting the pen name "Mark Twain" from an expression used by leadsmen on Mississippi steamboats. Under this name he published his first successful story, "Jim Smiley and His Jumping Frog," in 1865 in the *New York Saturday Press*. This later became the title story of *The Celebrated Jumping Frog of Calaveras County and Other Sketches* (1867), a collection that brought Clemens great popularity as a humorist. His reputation was increased with *The Innocents Abroad* (1869), an account of a trip to Europe.

Following his marriage to Olivia Langdon in 1870 and their relocation to Hartford, Connecticut, several years later, Clemens published a series of books that capitalized on a new interest in the southern and western United States. These included *Roughing It* (1872), an account of Twain's travels in Nevada, San Francisco, and the Sandwich Islands (Hawaii); *The Gilded Age* (1873; with Charles Dudley Warner), a novel mixing satire, romance, and sensationalism; the autobiographical *Life on the Mississippi* (1883), telling much about Twain's boyhood; and his two most famous novels, both based on his own childhood, *The Adventures of Tom Sawyer* (1876) and its informal sequel, *Adventures of Huckleberry Finn* (1885). *The Prince and the Pauper* (1882), in which the young King Edward VI of England (1537–1553) changes place with a boy of the streets, and *A Connecticut Yankee in King Arthur's Court* (1889) are two fantasies edged with social criticism and satire. Twain's Victorian audience enjoyed them as popular fiction.

The last two decades of Clemens's life brought significant changes and mark a distinct stage in his writing. Failed business enterprises and debts prompted him to move his family from the expensive home in Hartford to Europe in 1891. Determined to pay off his debts, Clemens embarked upon a worldwide lecture tour and wrote several popular books: *Tom Sawyer Abroad* (1894); *Pudd'nhead Wilson* (1894), a murder mystery set in a small Mississippi town; *Personal Recollections of Joan of Arc* (1896), an historical novel; and *Tom Sawyer, Detective* (1896). Personal tragedy beset the family in 1896 when Clemens's oldest daughter, Suzy, died of spinal meningitis and his youngest daughter, Jean, was diagnosed as an epileptic. In 1900 the Clemenses returned to the United States and settled in New York City. Clemens turned away from fiction in favor of public speaking (for which he was much sought after) and magazine articles and editorials. "Mark Twain" the humorist began to give way to the bitter satirist and outspoken social critic. He began to take seriously his self-appointed role of spokesman for the common man, and his audience largely approved. A collection of misanthropic tales and sketches, *The Man That Corrupted Hadleyburg* (1900), the bleak philosophical dialogue *What Is Man?* (1906), and the disturbing fantasy *The Mysterious Stranger* (published posthumously in 1916, in a much-edited version) were three of his last major works.

Jean's worsening epileptic condition (she died in 1909) and the death of Clemens's wife, Olivia, in 1904 cast a deepening shadow over the writer's last years. In 1906 he began to dictate his *Autobiography* to his secretary Albert Bigelow Paine. The book appeared in several editions following his death on April 21, 1910. ❖

Thematic and Structural Analysis

Mark Twain's *Huckleberry Finn* is an adventure story. It tells of the efforts of an adolescent boy from a small town in Missouri to escape both the brutality of his drunken father and the restrictions of his "sivilizing" surrogate parents. He is joined by a kind and superstitious runaway slave named Jim. Huck and Jim float down the Mississippi River on a large raft, and the various characters, situations, and places they encounter along the way form the narrative substance of the novel. They get themselves into every kind of trouble. They concoct stratagems and false identities to get themselves out of trouble. They form alliances with dubious characters. They are alternately betrayed and assisted. They sleep by day and travel by night. They pinch fruit and have countless narrow escapes. And they often simply sit back and talk and laugh and enjoy the lazy pleasures of life on a raft.

The sheer number of incidents makes it difficult to summarize *Huckleberry Finn,* but Twain does maintain a fairly consistent pattern of writing throughout the multiplicity of events. The whole story is spoken in the first person by Huck. At each stage of the journey, Huck usually offers his readers both a description of what happens and his own homespun reflections on the event's larger meaning or importance. It is in these reflections that Twain touches on his major themes, rendering most fully what has come to be seen as the special and lasting greatness of this novel—the colloquial, philosophical, self-deprecating, stubbornly boyish, provincial, sensitive, but always tough and realistic voice of Huckleberry Finn.

The **first chapter** serves to introduce us to the richness of this voice. Huck begins by reminding his readers of the ending of *The Adventures of Tom Sawyer,* the novel to which *Huckleberry Finn* is a sequel. He then describes his current situation. The Widow Douglass has adopted him, and Judge Thatcher, a kindly local magistrate, has promised to give Huck one dollar a day from interest on the money that he and Tom Sawyer recovered from "robbers" at the end of the previous book. Huck likes the money well enough but living with the Widow is a trial:

> The Widow Douglas, she took me for her son, and allowed she would sivilize me; but it was rough living in the house all the time, considering how dismal regular and decent the widow was in all her ways; and so when I couldn't stand it no longer, I lit out. I got into my old rags, and my sugar-hogshead again, and was free and satisfied. But Tom Sawyer, he hunted me up and said he was going to start a band of robbers, and I might join if I would go back to the widow and be respectable. So I went back.

This passage gives the flavor of Huck's distinctively slangy manner of narration. It also provides a preliminary glimpse of the novel's major theme—the conflict between "freedom" and "sivilization." Huck speaks here for the "primal," "instinctive," or simply "natural" part of the human personality that inevitably chafes against the "dismal" regularity of respectable middle-class living. But "lighting out" is not a simple matter. "Sivilization" has a powerful claim on Huck, and it continues to entangle him in its complex web of rules, manners, artifices, and conventions. It is consistent with Huck's hostility toward civilized constraints that he only agrees to come back to the Widow in order to qualify for Tom Sawyer's imaginary band of robbers. It is also consistent with Twain's ironic perspective that respectability and robbery are closely associated in this passage. Twain follows the eighteenth-century philosopher Jean-Jacques Rousseau in suggesting throughout the novel that civilization and culture corrupt rather than improve human beings. Huck and Jim are both happier and morally more admirable—"free and satisfied"—when they are out alone on the river, in close harmony with nature, spontaneously kind and generous, far from towns and authorities and "regular" ways.

But in **chapters one to four** at any rate Huck is stuck in a proper house, enduring the benevolent middle-class training of Miss Watson. She tries to cure him of his superstition, tells him about the Bible and saying grace, and scolds him when he sneaks out of the house at night to join Tom Sawyer and the gang and comes home with his clothes all muddy. Huck has no interest in the Bible—he "don't take no stock in dead peo-ple"—and he does not believe Miss Watson when she tells him you can get anything you want if you pray for it. "I tried it," he says simply, "there ain't nuthin in it." But he does begin to get used to sleeping in a bed, and he even gets to like going to school, where he is learning to read and write. When so much refinement becomes overwhelming he plays hooky, or sleeps in the woods for a night, or goes off on an imaginary raid with Tom and the gang. Initially the gang will not accept Huck because he does not have a family that they can murder if he betrays one of their members, but they relent when he offers them Miss Watson. For several months things swim along quite smoothly for Huck, until he turns over a saltcellar at breakfast and is prevented by Miss Watson from tossing a pinch over his shoulder. Bad luck arrives the next day when some ominous footprints with a cross in the left boot heel warn Huck that his no-good Pap is back in town.

Huck acts quickly. With characteristic canniness he suspects that his father has come to try to get his stash of money, and so he goes and tries to give the money to Judge Thatcher. Huck's fundamental lack of interest in material things is suggested by this gesture, but the kindly Judge senses that something is amiss and will only allow Huck to "sell" the money to him, so that he can legally protect it. Huck's next step is also characteristic; he consults the "nigger" Jim's hairball as to what his father's movements are likely to be. As interpreted by Jim after being fed a quarter, the hairball offers a hilarious mishmash of vague and contradictory predictions, but Huck feels nonetheless edified. Superstition plays the role of a sort of alternative culture in this novel. It structures the beliefs and behavior of "uncultured" or "uncivilized" characters such as Jim and Huck. Huck has far less faith in portents than Jim, but he notices over the course of the novel that Jim's apparently random fatalism often holds a grain of truth. In any case, when Huck returns to Miss Watson's house that night, he finds his long-absent Pap sitting in his room.

Chapters five to seven are dominated by the hateful figure of Huck's Pap. He is described as intimidating and physically repulsive. "His hair," Huck tells us, "was long and tangled and greasy, and hung down, and you could see his eyes shining through like he was behind vines." He is dressed in rags, he smells of liquor, and his skin is deathly pale—"white," Huck tells us, "white to make a body sick . . . tree toad white, a fish-belly white." His first words to his son are full of resentment for Huck's improved worldly position. He accuses Huck of feeling superior because of his "starchy" clothes and his school learning. He challenges Huck to read from one of the books in the room, and when Huck successfully reads to him about "General Washington and the wars" Pap knocks the book across the room. The liberty from tyrannous authority and the promise of self-improvement for which General Washington fought are denied to Huck as his father bitterly threatens him. "If I catch you in that school, I'll tan you good," Pap warns, "I'll learn people to bring up a boy to put on airs over his father."

Pap lives up to his harsh promise over the next few months. He stays in town in the hope of wresting Huck's money away from Judge Thatcher, and when this fails he forces Huck to get money for him. He uses the money to drink and carry on, and whenever he catches Huck on the way to school he thrashes him. The Widow Douglas and Judge Thatcher attempt to gain legal custody of Huck to protect him against his father, but a new judge rules against them on the grounds that it is important to keep families together. This judge even goes so far as to take Pap into his own home and try to rehabilitate him. This arrangement works for a little while; Pap seems to be improving until one night he sneaks out of the judge's house, buys a bottle and brings it back to his room, and then falls off the roof and breaks his arm as he attempts to sneak out again. The judge gives up at this point, saying this fellow could only be reformed "with a shotgun." Pap continues to hang around, however, drinking and passing in and out of jail. Finally, angered by the Widow's threats, Pap takes Huck three miles up the river to a small cabin in the Illinois woods.

Pap locks Huck in the cabin by day while he goes out and fishes and hunts for food. In the evenings Huck helps to cook, while his father drinks and occasionally beats him. If it were not for the beatings, Huck tells us with his usual adaptability, it would be a fine way to live. It is "kind of lazy and jolly" not having to study. After two months his clothes have become comfortably ragged and dirty again, and he loses all interest in going back to the town. But the beatings become intolerable, and when at one point Pap leaves Huck locked in the cabin for three days, Huck begins to plan an escape. He finds a saw and makes a hole in the wall of the cabin, which he then disguises. When Pap returns and sends him out the next evening to check the fishing lines, Huck catches an abandoned canoe coming down the river and hides it for future use. A few days later, after Pap has gone to town to sell some logs they have caught, Huck fills the canoe with provisions, bloodies the ax, and leaves clumps of his hair and pig's blood around the cabin to make it look as if he has been murdered. He then drags a sack of rocks down to the bank, leaving a trail to make it look as if his body were dumped in the river. He waits in the canoe, and when he sees Pap pass by on his way back home, he "lights out" for Jackson's Island and arrives there safely. Before fording the island, he sits for a moment and contemplates the "solemn" stillness of the big river that has brought him, for the moment, to freedom.

Huck's time on Jackson's Island (**ch. 8**) is one of several peaceful and pleasant interludes in the novel. In contrast to the regularity of life with Miss Watson and the fearfulness of life with Pap, life on the island is "powerful lazy and comfortable." Huck explores the island's spaces and tastes its food, and one day he has the unique experience of sitting and watching a boatload of familiar people—Tom Sawyer, Pap, Judge Thatcher, Aunt Polly, and others—passing back and forth "trying to make my carcass come to the top" by firing cannonballs into the river. Huck takes an odd pleasure in watching his friends search for his own dead body. Later that evening, however, he gets to feeling "lonesome" as he sets his lines, so he focuses on counting the stars. (Nature often takes the place of Huck's abandoned community in this novel.) His lonesomeness is soon assuaged, however, when he goes to investigate another campfire on the island and finds to his surprise the sleeping form of "Miss Watson's nigger"—Jim. Huck pipes out and says "Hello!" and Jim awakens in terror, believing that Huck must be a ghost. When Huck at last convinces him otherwise, Jim is delighted to see him, and they lay back and have a long talk. Huck tells Jim of his subterfuge at Pap's cabin, and Jim tells Huck, reluctantly, how he "ran off" to avoid being sold by Miss

Watson. Jim asks Huck to promise not to tell, and Huck agrees, but with some pangs of conscience. The thought that virtually everyone in his former community will despise him as "a low-down abolitionist" gives Huck pause, but his affection for Jim wins out for the moment. "That won't make no difference," he decides, and Jim and he spend a happy evening discussing wealth, stocks, luck, and "all kinds of signs." Jim assures Huck that one day he (Jim) is going to be rich because he has "hairy arms and a hairy breast."

The next day they set up camp in a cool, dry cave on a ridge (**ch. 9**). Because Jim has seen a sign, they decide to carry their traps up the ridge and store them in the cave. That evening, sure enough, a ferocious rainstorm sweeps the island. They sit in the shelter of their cave and watch the storm, and Huck's description of it is one of the most striking of the novel's many beautiful evocations of the power of nature:

> Directly it begun to rain, and it rained like all fury, too, and I never see the wind blow so. It was one of these regular summer storms. It would get so dark that it looked all blue-black out-side, and lovely; and the rain would thrash along by so thick that the trees off a little ways looked dim and spider-webby; and here would come a blast of wind that would bend the trees down and turn up the pale underside of the leaves; and then a perfect ripper of a gust would follow along and set the branches to tossing their arms as if they was just wild; and next, when it was just about the bluest and blackest—*fst!* it was as bright as glory and you'd have a little glimpse of tree-tops a-plunging about, away off yonder in the storm, hundreds of yards further than you could see before; dark as sin again in a second, and how you'd hear the thunder let go with an awful crash and then rumbling, grumbling, tumbling down the sky towards the under side of the world, like rolling empty barrels down stairs, where it's long stairs, and they bounce a good deal, you know.

The writing here is a powerful mixture of deep feeling, care-fully paced language, and subtle and precise observation. But Huck's familiar colloquial style—with such phrases as "a perfect ripper" or "away off yonder"—keeps the passage from sound-ing unduly elevated or pretentious, reminding the reader that the sensitive observer of this scene is a lonesome and untu-tored adolescent. Huck is capable of an intimate closeness and familiarity with nature that he cannot seem to manage with any of the people in the book, except for Jim. Perhaps the storm's fury expresses some of his own suppressed anger toward his brutal father. Or perhaps its wildness reflects his own deep resistance to taming. Whatever the case, it is clear that Huck achieves a peace of mind in beholding the glories of nature that he never finds in civilized society. "Jim, this is nice," Huck says, "I wouldn't want to be nowhere else but here."

Similarly idyllic moments are soon achieved out on the river. Jim and Huck abandon Jackson's Island in a hurry after Huck learns from a woman across the river that bounty hunters are pursuing Jim and have seen his campfire on the island. Using an abandoned section of lumber raft that they snatched when the water was high, they float down to a towhead sixteen or seventeen miles below the village. Here they spend a happy day lying in hiding and watching "the rafts and steamboats spin down the Missouri shore, and up-bound steamboats fight the big river down the middle."

At dusk, Jim builds a wigwam on the raft to protect their things and themselves from the hot sun and the rain, and they set off again. The wigwam functions as a symbol of natural as opposed to conventional domesticity, and their nocturnal schedule sets them in opposition to conventional notions of time. An almost religious peacefulness sets in: "We catched fish, and talked, and we took a swim now and then to keep off sleepiness. It was kind of solemn, drifting down the big still river, lying on our backs looking up at the stars, and we didn't even feel like talking loud, and it warn't often that we laughed, only a little bit of low chuckle. We had mighty good weather, as a general thing, and nothing ever happened to us at all, that night, nor the next, nor the next" (**ch. 12**).

They do eventually get into some trouble when against Jim's better judgment they board a shipwrecked steamboat occupied by a group of murderous thieves, losing the raft in the process. But even this works out well when they manage not only to recover the raft, but capture the thieves' money and supplies, which include a number of books. They find themselves rich—just as Jim predicted—and they spend a few pleasant afternoons reading the books, talking, and "having a general good time." Huck's efforts to teach Jim about European aristocracy offer a hilarious example of the blind leading the blind, and they afford Twain an opportunity to poke some sly fun at one of his favorite targets.

The young travelers' ultimate plan is to proceed south to where the Ohio River meets the Mississippi at Cairo. There they intend to sell the raft and board a steamboat north up the Ohio into the free territories. But this strategy proves difficult to execute. On the second of what they believe will be a three-night journey to Cairo (**ch. 15**) a thick fog settles over the river. Huck paddles ahead in the canoe to try to secure a spot on the shore, but he soon loses his bearings, and Jim does not respond to his "whoops" as he tries to return to the raft. They are reunited the following evening under a clear night sky, but in the meantime they have unknowingly passed Cairo and their route to freedom on the Ohio. Huck and Jim's previously harmonious friendship also hits a snag at this point. Jim was asleep when Huck rediscovered the raft after the night of fog, and Huck crept aboard and pretended to have been there all the time. When Jim wakes up and embraces him and carries on about the troubles of the night before, Huck insists that Jim must have been dreaming, saying he had been there sleeping next to him the whole time. Jim is momentarily taken in but then becomes furious with Huck when he realizes he has been tricked. He tells Huck that his heart was "mos broke bekase you wuz los," and that when he found him again he cried for joy and was so thankful that he could have kissed Huck's foot. "En all you wuz thinkin 'bout wuz how you could make a fool uv ol Jim wid a lie. Dat truck day is trash; en trash is what people is dat puts dirt on de head er dey fren's en makes 'em ashamed." Huck feels bad immediately and realizes that Jim is right, but it takes him fifteen minutes to overcome his resistance to "humbling myself to a nigger." His innate decency soon wins out, however, and he apologizes. Huck's reflection on the event suggests his basic good-heartedness: "I didn't do him no more mean tricks, and I wouldn't done that one if I'd a knowed it would make him feel that way."

Huck's feelings for Jim, however, are soon tested further. As they proceed down the river with no sign of Cairo, they begin to wonder if they have passed it by. Huck decides to take the canoe ashore and inquire about their location. But as he prepares to depart he senses Jim's growing excitement about what he believes to be his imminent freedom, and this gives Huck pause. All the disapproval associated in the South with helping to free a slave begins to weigh on Huck. He thinks about how generous Miss Watson had always been to him, and he begins to think that he is thanklessly stealing from her. An oppressive sense of guilt overwhelms him—"I got to feeling so mean and so miserable I most wished I was dead" (**ch. 16**). He resolves that at the first opportunity he will tell the authorities on shore of Jim's identity and whereabouts. This makes him feel a great deal better, and when they spot a light on shore he prepares to execute his plan. Jim, on the other hand, believes that the light is Cairo, and he begins to thank Huck effusively for all he has done for him. He tells Huck gratefully that he is "the best friend I ever had," that he could never have become free without him, and that he is "the only White gel'man that ever kept his promise to Jim." Huck "freezes" and feels "sick" as he hears these glowing words, but he resolves again to do what he now feels he must do. Much to his own surprise, however, when he almost immediately runs into two men looking for escaped "niggers" who ask him if the man on the raft is white or black, he hears himself say that Jim is white. And when they suggest that they will go check, Huck protects Jim further by implying cleverly that he has smallpox, scaring the men away. Jim overhears Huck's protective ruse and again thanks Huck effusively when he returns to the raft. For his part, Huck merely feels "bad and low." He feels he is too weak to turn Jim in. It is too much trouble to try to do the right thing, he reflects resignedly, so he "won't bother no more about it" and just "do what is handiest at the time."

The novel's central theme is contained in the irony that Huck feels ashamed of precisely those actions that make him most noble. In commenting on *Adventures of Huckleberry Finn,* Mark Twain referred to it as "a book of mine where a sound heart and a deformed conscience come into collision and conscience suffers defeat." Huck's conscience has been "deformed" by the culture of slavery in which he grows up. Twain is offering a very subtle picture of how the corrupt values of such a culture perpetuate themselves by working themselves into a child's deepest emotional and mental responses.

All the authority figures Huck knows—Miss Watson, Judge Thatcher, Tom Sawyer, and certainly Pap—would condemn him for treating Jim as anything other than property, and their voices would have become a deeply rooted part of his personality. The difficulty of ignoring or overcoming these voices is in many ways the subject of the novel. Ironically, it is precisely those qualities in Huck that make him uneasy with civilized norms that finally make it possible for him to reach a higher level of civility than most of the other characters in the book. Because Huck is unusually open to nature and experience and, like countless American immigrants and pioneers, is willing to "light out" in search of something new, he is able to liberate himself from corrupting conventions. This is the moral meaning of his and Jim's passage down the river. They are both liberating themselves from slavery, and the solvent of their chains is a "sound heart"—the spontaneous kindness and respect and loyalty they come to feel toward one another as they journey to freedom.

Huck undergoes a similar crisis again toward the end of the novel, but in the meantime he and Jim endure a number of increasingly dangerous adventures. Morning light reveals a mixture of clear Ohio water with the Mississippi muddy, confirming once and for all that they have indeed passed Cairo and are headed south toward Arkansas. They decide to abandon the raft and paddle upstream in their canoe, but their canoe is stolen. They then decide to continue down on the raft until they can buy a canoe, but on that evening the raft is mowed down by a steamship. Huck dives deep to avoid the ship's wheels, and when he surfaces there is no sign of Jim. He goes ashore and soon finds himself being graciously taken care of by a well-worn, well-dressed, well-spoken, and well-off family by the name of Grangerford. Everything about these folks smacks of refinement; they are, as Huck puts it, "a handsome lot of quality" (**ch. 18**). But Twain again raises questions about the depth of such civility as we find out that for generations these exquisite people have been involved in a ferociously bloody feud with the Sheperdsons, a neighboring aristocratic family. Huck spends some pleasant time living in the Grangerfords' elegant house, riding and hunting with one of the sons, Buck. He develops a soft spot for one of the daughters, Sophia, and he even locates Jim when some of the household slaves lead him quietly to a nearby hidden cabin where they have been sheltering and feeding him. Jim nearly cries when he sees Huck, and he tells him that he is working on repairing the damaged raft. This soon proves useful when Huck places himself in the midst of the rekindled feud by unwittingly delivering a message that facilitates Sophia's elopement with one of the hated Sheperdsons. Huck is sickened and frightened by the pointless violence, and he and Jim flee. They are greatly relieved to get back on the river. As Huck says, "You feel mighty free and easy and comfortable on a raft" (**ch. 18**).

Their ease does not last long, however, as they are soon taken up by two con men. Huck quickly sees through their efforts to present themselves as fallen European royalty, but with his characteristic survivor's passivity he deems it wisest to play along with them for the time being. For the next eleven chapters (**chs. 19–29**), one of the longest sections of the book, Huck and Jim reluctantly join with the King and the Duke as they go from village to village trying out various scams. They preach and pass the hat at camp meetings, perform confused pieces of Shakespearean tragedy, sell themselves as experts in phrenology, or do whatever "missionarying," "mesmering," "doctoring," or fortune-telling they think will most effectively separate their rural victims from their money. They usually have some success in the beginning until the people of a town catch on to them and chase them out. Twain uses their forays as an opportunity for a sort of satiric survey of the narrow, provincial, sentimental, and shallow aspects of life in the rural South. Finally, in their most elaborate scam, the King and the Duke attempt to present themselves as the rightful inheritors of the money and property of a well-to-do man who dies. Using fake accents, they manage to convince the man's daughters and friends that they are his English kin. They come very close to making off with all his wealth until Huck surreptitiously throws a wrench into their schemes. The real English kin show up, and the King and Duke narrowly escape being lynched. Their last treacherous act is to sell Jim to bounty hunters for forty dollars.

Huck is heartbroken at losing Jim, and he quickly finds out where he has been taken. But he must again engage in a long fight with his conscience before he can dedicate himself to trying to liberate him. The voices of corrupt authority return, and it is only when Huck reflects on his life with Jim on the river—"and I see Jim before me, all the time, in the day, and in the night-time, sometimes moonlight, sometimes storms, and we a floating along, talking, and singing, and laughing" (**ch. 31**)—that he tears up the note he has written to Miss Watson telling her of "her nigger's" whereabouts and rededicates himself to obtaining Jim's freedom. This, Huck's second explicit battle with his conscience, is the moral climax of the novel.

Hereafter, the plot takes some rather surprising and elaborate turns. Huck discovers that Jim's guardians are none other than Tom Sawyer's aunt and uncle, and Tom himself arrives on a journey down from Missouri. Never having seen Tom before, his aunt and uncle are deceived by the boys into believing that Huck is Tom and that Tom is their own nephew Sid, and they are both warmly welcomed. Huck recruits Tom to the task of freeing Jim and, guided by Tom's reading of Alexandre Dumas and Sir Walter Scott, they soon engineer an outrageously elaborate plan of action. The plan misfires and leaves Tom, much to his delight, with a bullet in his leg. Jim, who gallantly stayed with Tom when he was wounded, is recaptured and nearly hung as an example to other slaves. But he is then released again when Tom Sawyer reveals to everyone's surprise that Miss Watson had died two months ago and freed Jim in her will. Tom's Aunt Polly arrives and confirms his statements. When asked why he did not speak up earlier, Tom says boyishly that he hoped to have some adventures with Jim. For his part, Jim is too overjoyed to worry about the details and attributes his good luck to his hairy breast. "Signs is signs," he says to Huck.

Huck is delighted at Jim's freedom, but it doesn't change his plans. He closes the novel with a classic statement of stubborn American self-reliance: "I reckon I got to light out for the Territory ahead of the rest, because Aunt Sally she's going to adopt me and sivilize me and I can't stand it. I been there before." ✤

—Neal Dolan
Harvard University

List of Characters

Huckleberry Finn is a mischievous, self-reliant, and good-hearted adolescent. His efforts to get away from his brutal father and his too-genteel surrogate mother are the subject of the novel. He takes up with a runaway slave named Jim, with whom he floats down the Mississippi River on a raft, encountering a host of adventures along the way. He forms a close friendship with Jim but struggles with his conscience over whether to help him to freedom or turn him in. The story is told from Huck's point of view, and his narrative voice is a remarkable mixture of bad grammar, slang, homespun wisdom, and lyrical attentiveness to nature.

Jim, at the start of the novel, is the house slave of Miss Watson, Huck's surrogate mother. He runs away when he hears that he is going to be sold and joins Huck in a long flight down the Mississippi. Jim is superstitious, kind, and extremely loyal to Huck. He protects Huck from the knowledge of his father's death, he often takes Huck's shift on the raft to allow Huck extra sleep, and toward the end of the novel he risks his very freedom to tend to Tom Sawyer's wound. He is eventually freed by Miss Watson in her will.

Pap is Huck's father. He is drunken, violent, unkempt, and intolerant. He neglects Huck completely until he hears that Huck has found some money, whereupon he attempts to get it from him by threatening and beating him. Huck escapes from him by making it look as if he (Huck) has been murdered. We find out at the end of the novel that Pap himself was murdered after Huck left him.

Tom Sawyer is Huck's middle-class friend and partner in various imaginary and real adventures. His fanciful style of mischief contrasts vividly with Huck's down-to-earth pragmatism. Huck nevertheless looks up to Tom because he is "respectable," intelligent, and educated. Tom draws upon adventure novels as models for all his activities, most notably his elaborate effort to help Huck free Jim toward the end of the book.

The King and the Duke are audacious con men who take up with Huck and Jim on their journey down the river and embroil them in many scams. They pass as exiled European royalty, actors, missionaries, doctors, teachers, phrenologists, and experts of various kinds. They are nearly killed when they attempt to pass as the beneficiaries of a wealthy dead man's will. They eventually betray Huck and Jim by selling Jim, and Huck last sees them tarred and feathered and ridden out of town on a rail.

Miss Watson is a gentle elderly lady who adopts Huck and makes the mistake of trying to "sivilize" him. Huck appreciates her kindness toward him, but he cannot bear her insistence on punctuality, starchy clothes, and proper table manners. Jim is initially her house slave, but she eventually frees him in her will.

The Grangerfords are a handsome and elegant aristocratic family who take Huck in at one point on his journey. In the southern tradition, they are extremely hospitable to Huck, especially the daughter Sophia and the son Buck, but their deadly feud with the Sheperdsons eventually forces Huck to flee.

Sherburn is a brave and violent man who shoots down a rival in the streets of one of the villages visited by Huck and the con-men. He then stands up single-handedly to a cowardly mob of men clamoring for blood. He represents a kind of individualistic rough justice.

Doctor Robinson is one of the rare men of genuine reason and learning whom Huck meets on his travels. He sees through the King and the Duke in their efforts to con the Wilkes family.

Uncle Silas and Aunt Sally Phelps are Tom Sawyer's aunt and uncle. They are the owners of the Arkansas farm where Jim is first imprisoned and then liberated by Tom and Huck. Aunt Sally is kind and maternal, and Uncle Silas is described as a kind and innocent man who is sincerely religious.

Aunt Polly is another of Tom's aunts. She arrives from Missouri at the end of the novel, confirms Jim's freedom, and reveals the true identity of Tom and Huck to the Phelps. ❖

Critical Views

[The following review, which was published anonymously, has been attributed to Brander Matthews (1852–1929), an important American critic, editor, and novelist. Matthews wrote many volumes, including *An Introduction to the Study of American Literature* (1896) and *The Development of the Drama* (1903). He was a vigorous proponent of the uniqueness of American English. In this review, Matthews stresses the skill with which Twain has portrayed the sensations of a teenage boy.]

Huckleberry Finn is autobiographic; it is a tale of boyish adventure along the Mississippi river told as it appeared to Huck Finn. There is not in *Huckleberry Finn* any one scene quite as funny as those in which Tom Sawyer gets his friends to whitewash the fence for him, and then uses the spoils thereby acquired to attain the highest situation of the Sunday school the next morning. Nor is there any distinction quite as thrilling as that awful moment in the cave when the boy and the girl are lost in the darkness, and when Tom Sawyer suddenly sees a human hand bearing a light, and then finds that the hand is the hand of Indian Joe, his one mortal enemy; we have always thought that the vision of the hand in the cave in *Tom Sawyer* is one of the very finest things in the literature of adventure since Robinson Crusoe first saw a single footprint in the sand of the seashore. But though *Huckleberry Finn* may not quite reach these two highest points of *Tom Sawyer,* we incline to the opinion that the general level of the later story is perhaps higher than that of the earlier. For one thing, the skill with which the character of Huck Finn is maintained is marvellous. We see everything through his eyes—and they are his eyes and not a pair of Mark Twain's spectacles. And the comments on what he sees are his comments—the comments of an ignorant, superstitious, sharp, healthy boy, brought up as Huck Finn had been brought up; they are not speeches put into his mouth by the author. One of the most artistic things in the book—and that

Mark Twain is a literary artist of a very high order all who have considered his later writings critically cannot but confess—one of the most artistic things in *Huckleberry Finn* is the sober self-restraint with which Mr. Clemens lets Huck Finn set down, without any comment at all, scenes which would have afforded the ordinary writer matter for endless moral and political and sociological disquisition. We refer particularly to the account of the Grangerford-Shepherdson feud, and of the shooting of Boggs by Colonel Sherburn. Here are two incidents of the rough old life of the South-Western States, and of the Mississippi Valley forty or fifty years ago, of the old life which is now rapidly passing away under the influence of advancing civilization and increasing commercial prosperity, but which has not wholly disappeared even yet, although a slow revolution in public sentiment is taking place. The Grangerford-Shepherdson feud is a vendetta as deadly as any Corsican could wish, yet the parties to it were honest, brave, sincere, good Christian people, probably people of deep religious sentiment. Not the less we see them taking their guns to church, and, when occasion serves, joining in what is little better than a general massacre. The killing of Boggs by Colonel Sherburn is told with equal sobriety and truth; and the later scene in which Colonel Sherburn cows and lashes the mob which has set out to lynch him is one of the most vigorous bits of writing Mark Twain has done.

In *Tom Sawyer* we saw Huckleberry Finn from the outside; in the present volume we see him from the inside. He is almost as much a delight to any one who has been a boy as was Tom Sawyer. But only he or she who has been a boy can truly enjoy this record of his adventures, and of his sentiments and of his sayings. Old maids of either sex will wholly fail to understand him or to like him, or to see his significance and his value. Like Tom Sawyer, Huck Finn is a genuine boy; he is neither a girl in boy's clothes like many of the modern heroes of juvenile fiction, nor is he a "little man," a full-grown man cut down; he is a boy, just a boy, only a boy. And his ways and modes of thought are boyish. As Mr. F. Anstey understands the English boy, and especially the English boy of the middle classes, so Mark Twain understands the American boy, and especially the American boy of the Mississippi Valley of forty or fifty years ago. The contrast between Tom Saywer, who is the child of respectable parents, decently brought up, and Huckleberry Finn, who is the child of the town drunkard, not brought up at all, is made distinct by a hundred artistic touches, not the least natural of which is Huck's constant reference to Tom as his ideal of what a boy should be. When Huck escapes from the cabin where his drunken and worthless father had confined him, carefully manufacturing a mass of very circumstantial evidence to prove his own murder by robbers, he cannot help saying, "I did wish Tom Sawyer was there, I knowed he would take an interest in this kind of business, and throw in the fancy touches. Nobody could spread himself like Tom Sawyer in such a thing as that." Both boys have their full share of boyish imagination; and Tom Sawyer, being given to books, lets his imagination run on robbers and pirates and genies, with a perfect understanding with himself that, if you want to get fun out of this life, you must never hesitate to make believe very hard; and, with Tom's youth and health, he never finds it hard to make believe and to be a pirate at will, or to summon an attendant spirit, or to rescue a prisoner from the deepest dungeon 'neath the castle moat. But in Huck this imagination has turned to superstition; he is a walking repository of the juvenile folklore of the Mississippi Valley—a folklore partly traditional among the white settlers, but largely influenced by intimate association with the negroes.

—Brander Matthews, [Review of *Adventures of Huckleberry Finn*], *Saturday Review* (London), 31 January 1885, pp. 153–54

ANDREW LANG ON THE REALISM OF *HUCKLEBERRY FINN*

[Andrew Lang (1844–1912) was a prolific Scottish novelist, poet, and critic. He is today perhaps best known for a series of fairy tale collections in which each volume is named after a color, such as *The Blue Fairy Book* (1889). He also wrote a number of whimsical critical essays, including *Letters to Dead Authors* (1886) and

Adventures among Books (1901). In this extract, Lang praises the faithfulness and lack of "partisanship" with which Twain has portrayed both the characters and the setting of his novel.]

What is it that we want in a novel? We want a vivid and original picture of life; we want character naturally displayed in action, and if we get the excitement of adventure into the bargain, and that adventure possible and plausible, I so far differ from the newest school of criticism as to think that we have additional cause for gratitude. If, moreover, there is an unstrained sense of humour in the narrator, we have a masterpiece and *Huckleberry Finn* is nothing less. Once more, if the critics are right who think that art should so far imitate nature as to leave things at loose ends, as it were, not pursuing events to their conclusions, even here *Huckleberry Finn* should satisfy them. It is the story of the flight down the Mississippi of a white boy and a runaway slave. The stream takes them through the fringes of life on the riverside; they pass feuds and murders of men, and towns full of homicidal loafers, and are intermingled with the affairs of families, and meet friends whom they would wish to be friends always. But the current carries them on: they leave the murders unavenged, the lovers in full flight; the friends they lose for ever; we do not know, any more than in reality we would know, 'what became of them all.' They do not return, as in novels, and narrate their later adventures.

As to the truth of the life described, the life in little innocent towns, the religion, the Southern lawlessness, the feuds, the lynchings, only persons who have known this changed world can say if it be truly painted, but it looks like the very truth, like an historical document. Already *Huckleberry Finn* is an historical novel, and more valuable, perhaps, to the historian than *Uncle Tom's Cabin*, for it was written without partisanship, and without 'a purpose.' The drawing of character seems to be admirable, unsurpassed in its kind. By putting the tale in the mouth of the chief actor, Huck, Mark Twain was enabled to give it a seriousness not common in his work, and to abstain from comment. Nothing can be more true and more humorous than the narrative of this outcast boy, with a heart naturally good, with a conscience torn between the teachings of his world about slavery and the promptings of his nature. In one point Mark Twain is Homeric, probably without knowing it. In the *Odyssey*, Odysseus frequently tells a false tale about himself, to account for his appearance and position when disguised on his own island. He shows extraordinary fertility and appropriateness of invention, wherein he is equalled by the feigned tales of Huckleberry Finn. The casual characters met on the way are masterly: the woman who detects Huck in a girl's dress; the fighting families of Shepherdson and Grangerford; the homicidal Colonel Sherburne, who cruelly shoots old Boggs, and superbly quells the mob of would-be lynchers; the various old aunts and uncles; the negro Jim; the two wandering impostors; the hateful father of Huck himself. Then Huck's compliment to Miss Mary Jane, whom he thought of afterwards 'a many and a many million times,' how excellent it is! 'In my opinion she had more sand in her than any girl I ever see; in my opinion she was just full of sand. It sounds like flattery, but it ain't no flattery. And when it comes to beauty—and goodness, too—she lays over them all.' No novel has better touches of natural description; the starlit nights on the great river, the storms, the whole landscape, the sketches of little rotting towns, of the woods, of the cotton-fields, are simple, natural, and visible to the mind's eye. The story, to be sure, ends by lapsing into burlesque, when Tom Sawyer insists on freeing the slave whom he knows to be free already, in a manner accordant with 'the best authorities.' But even the burlesque is redeemed by Tom's real unconscious heroism. There are defects of taste, or passages that to us seem deficient in taste, but the book remains a nearly flawless gem of romance and of humour. The world appreciates it, no doubt, but 'cultured critics' are probably unaware of its singular value. A two-shilling novel by Mark Twain, with an ugly picture on the cover, 'has no show,' as Huck might say, and the great American novel has escaped the eyes of those who watch to see this new planet swim into their ken. And will Mark Twain never write such another? One is enough for him to live by, and for our gratitude, but not enough for our desire.

—Andrew Lang, "The Art of Mark Twain," *Illustrated London News*, 14 February 1891, p. 222

❖

[Carl Van Doren (1885–1950), older brother of Mark Van Doren, was a biographer and critic who wrote books on such writers as Thomas Love Peacock (1911), James Branch Cabell (1925), and Sinclair Lewis (1933). He was also the managing editor of *The Cambridge History of American Literature* (1917–21). In this extract, Van Doren emphasizes the humor of *Huckleberry Finn* and shows how it represents a continuity with Twain's earlier works of humor, satire, and burlesque.]

A restless traveler, ⟨Twain⟩ wandered over America and Europe, and he lectured around the earth. Enough of a reader to find out what he wanted to know about the past, he went through it exactly as he went through the present. He saw everything with the eye of innocence. An American Adam, he did not know or care that the beasts in the garden had been named by earlier Adams and had traditional reputations for goodness and badness, ugliness or beauty. Mark Twain spoke like a new Adam, calling new names. The world, sluggish with opinions held by rote, heard him, suddenly perceived how right he was, and laughed.

No man of genius could find so much to laugh at without finding also much to hate. Mark Twain's hatred of cruelty and stupidity, of oppression and superstition and hypocrisy, lengthened the thrust of his ridicule. His burlesque of knightly life under King Arthur and his tender chronicle of Joan of Arc were at the same time savage forays against ancient wrongs. Many of his comments on contemporary life were stern and bitter. Yet the solid body of his work rose from his own memory of his real or imagined adventures. The older the memory the better the story.

In *Huckleberry Finn,* the high point of his achievement, he reached back to the Mississippi of his boyhood, when the great river had bounded his life and flowed through his imagination. He took Huck Finn from his native village to drift, as the actual Mark Twain had not been allowed to do, to freedom on the Mississippi. With a fugitive slave for his companion, Huck must not be seen. He must travel most of the time by night and lie and steal his way. The river is his universe of comedy and tragedy. Telling Huck's story, Mark Twain had small need of exaggeration. The Mississippi, as he remembered it and his boyish idea of it, was more than any man could make up. The truth would do.

Perhaps he scarcely noticed that his memory had been touched by grandeur during creative years. Nor did this grandeur put out wings and lose itself in a void like that which had hovered over Melville's Pacific. Ahab had been metaphysical and mad. Huck was green, sly, and sane. Mark Twain had to cut the river to fit the understanding of his hero. He could be eloquent about it only in words which Huck might have used. As Huck's dimensions gave the story its form, so his nature colored its materials. Seen through him, as narrator, the episodes have a double innocence and are doubly comic. Laughter springs from both the story and the story-teller.

Huckleberry Finn is Mark Twain in his simplest words. It is the folk-tale of the American people told in their language by their Man Laughing. It is the epic of America's happy memory as *Moby-Dick* is the epic of America's unquiet mind.

—Carl Van Doren, *What Is American Literature?* (New York: William Morrow, 1935), pp. 81–84

JAMES T. FARRELL ON HUCK FINN AND TOM SAWYER

[James T. Farrell (1904–1979) is best known as the author of the Studs Lonigan trilogy (*Young Lonigan,* 1932; *The Young Manhood of Studs Lonigan,* 1934; *Judgment Day,* 1935), a series of novels that utilized the literary technique of naturalism, or a grim portrayal of the harsh realities of working-class life. Farrell also wrote a small number of essays and reviews. In this extract, Farrell compares the characters of Huck Finn and Tom Sawyer, concluding that Tom is a romantic while Huck is a realist.]

It is significant that Tom and Huck are boys rather than men, and therefore the more easily surrounded with an aura of optimism. Whereas the adults in their Mississippi village look down on Negro slaves as if they were not human beings, Tom and Huck tend even to envy them. Less influenced by the village standards, they can associate more freely with Negroes than can adults. And consequently, Huck is able to come to grips with the moral problems posed by the very existence of the institution of chattel slavery. Huck lives like a pioneer, like a squatter in miniature. His respect for property rights is almost nil. To filch watermelons and other food, to "borrow" someone else's canoe, to ignore conventions and moral standards— none of this troubles his conscience. But when it so happens that property rights involve another human being, then he faces a moral problem. This problem cuts into the heart of pre–Civil War America. And Huck resolves the problem by deciding he will have to help the Negro, Jim, even at the risk of eternal damnation. To help a Negro slave escape is a "low-down thing to do." A person "don't want to take no consequence of it." The more this problem troubles Huck, "the more my conscience kept grinding me, and the more wicked and low-down and ornery I got to feeling." He tries to soften his conscience by convincing himself that he was brought up "wicked." He tries to pray, "but one can't pray a lie." He plans to write Jim's owner a letter and thereby save himself from this evil. He can't. The humanity of Jim outweighs the moral code of Huck's environment. Huck makes a moral choice: he helps Jim to escape. He is in it for good, so he will go "the whole hog." Here we see Huck affirming the value of a living human being of the present as against the claims justified in an institution of the past. And this affirmation is the very core of Mark Twain's own sense of the worth of human beings. To continue: Tom and Huck are shrewd, daring, ingenious. These are traits that Mark Twain admired. Tom Sawyer is the type of boy who could grow up to be a Pudd'nhead Wilson. The resourcefulness of Huck parallels that of the Connecticut Yankee. Thus, when Tom and Huck outwit adults, we must not interpret these passages merely as humor. Through his two unspoiled boys Twain forcefully emphasized his own attitudes and values.

The Adventures of Tom Sawyer is a boy's book. Its sequel, The Adventures of Huckleberry Finn, is an adult's novel. However, the two books should not be considered separately, for Tom and Huck are contrasts. Tom is a romantic; Huck, a realist. At first this temperamental difference seems paradoxical when we think of the circumstances of their lives. Tom lives a regular life. Cared for by his Aunt Polly, he is an accepted member of the community. He is sent to school, is taken to church and Sunday school, and he goes on picnics with other children whose parents also live orderly lives. He becomes the boyhood sweetheart of Becky Thatcher, whose father is one of the leading figures in the village. Tom seeks to escape from regularity by romanticism. He feeds on detective and adventure stories (in fact, the very characterization of Tom constitutes a satire on this form of writing), and he strives to translate what he reads into the real world around him. Huck, on the contrary, is a realist living under romantic circumstances. There is no order in his life. He is a child of whim and impulse, heedless of authority and convention. The other boys are warned by their parents and their teacher not to associate with him. But Huck represents common sense as opposed to romanticism. Since his problems are of a life-and-death character, he must be a realist in order to survive. Tom's real problems are settled for him, so that he is more concerned with those of his imagination. Huck, equally adventurous, cannot afford the luxury of romanticism.

As a result of these differences, Huck appears to be more mature than Tom, although they are of the same age. At the conclusion of The Adventures of Huckleberry Finn, Tom seems to be the same charming boy he was when we first met him, while Huck has developed and grown in character, having acquired a clearer and purer sense of moral values. It is this fact that explains the difference between the two books—revealed also in the humor, which is much more pointed in the second novel. There was usually a devastating attack behind the playfulness and humor of Mark Twain. The extravaganza, the burlesque included in the saga of Huck Finn is pointed at the old South and cuts to the heart of a whole society. The sharpest humor in The Adventures of Tom Sawyer strikes less deeply; it is directed at adventure writing and at the school system of the period. But, taken together, both boys stand in contrast to "the damned human race."

—James T. Farrell, "Mark Twain's *Huckleberry Finn* and *Tom Sawyer*" (1943), *The League of Frightened Philistines and Other Papers* (New York: Vanguard Press, 1945), pp. 26–29

LIONEL TRILLING ON HUCK'S ATTITUDE TOWARD SLAVERY

[Lionel Trilling (1905–1975), one of the most significant American critics of the twentieth century, was the author of many works of criticism, including *The Opposing Self* (1955) and *Sincerity and Authenticity* (1972). In the following extract, taken from his important volume, *The Liberal Imagination* (1950), Trilling ponders what Huck Finn's views of slavery actually are, concluding that his helping to free Jim is not a result of an abstract belief that slavery is wrong but a function of his personal devotion to a friend.]

And if Huck and Jim on the raft do indeed make a community of saints, it is because they do not have an ounce of pride between them. Yet this is not perfectly true, for the one disagreement they ever have is over a matter of pride. It is on the occasion when Jim and Huck have been separated by the fog. Jim has mourned Huck as dead, and then, exhausted, has fallen asleep. When he awakes and finds that Huck has returned, he is overjoyed, but Huck convinces him that he has only dreamed the incident, that there has been no fog, no separation, no chase, no reunion, and then allows him to make an elaborate "interpretation" of the dream he now believes he has had. Then the joke is sprung, and in the growing light of the dawn Huck points to the debris of leaves on the raft and the broken oar.

> Jim looked at the trash, and then looked at me, and back at the trash again. He had got the dream fixed so strong in his head that he couldn't seem to shake it loose and get the facts back into its place again right away. But when he did get the thing

straightened around he looked at me steady without ever smiling, and says:

"What do dey stan' for? I'se gwyne to tell you. When I got all wore out wid work, en wid de callin' for you, en went to sleep, my heart wuz mos' broke bekase you wuz los', en I didn' k'yer no mo' what became er me en de raf'. En when I wake up en fine you back agin, all safe en soun', de tears come, en I could a got down on my knees en kiss yo' foot, I's so thankful. En all you wuz thinkin' 'bout wuz how you could make a fool uv ole Jim wid a lie. Dat truck dah is *trash*; en trash is what people is dat puts dirt on de head er dey fren's en makes 'em ashamed."

Then he got up slow and walked to the wigwam, and went in there without saying anything but that.

The pride of human affection has been touched, one of the few prides that has any true dignity. And at its utterance, Huck's one last dim vestige of pride of status, his sense of his position as a white man, wholly vanishes: "It was fifteen minutes before I could work myself up to go and humble myself to a nigger; but I done it, and I warn't sorry for it afterwards either."

The incident is the beginning of the moral testing and development which a character so morally sensitive as Huck's must inevitably undergo. And it becomes an heroic character when, on the urging of affection, Huck discards the moral code he has always taken for granted and resolves to help Jim in his escape from slavery. The intensity of his struggle over the act suggests how deeply he is involved in the society which he rejects. The satiric brilliance of the episode lies, of course, in Huck's solving his problem not by doing "right" but by doing "wrong." He has only to consult his conscience, the conscience of a Southern boy in the middle of the last century, to know that he ought to return Jim to slavery. And as soon as he makes the decision according to conscience and decides to inform on Jim, he has all the warmly gratifying emotions of conscious virtue. "Why, it was astonishing, the way I felt as light as a feather right straight off, and my troubles all gone. . . . I felt good and all washed clean of sin for the first time I had ever felt so in my life, and I knowed I could pray now." And when at last he finds that he cannot endure his decision but must sacrifice the comforts of the pure heart and help Jim in his escape, it is not because he has acquired any new ideas about slavery—he believes that he detests Abolitionists; he himself answers when he is asked if the explosion of a steamboat boiler had hurt anyone, "No'm, killed a nigger," and of course finds nothing wrong in the responsive comment, "Well, it's lucky because sometimes people do get hurt." Ideas and ideals can be of no help to him in his moral crisis. He no more condemns slavery than Tristram and Lancelot condemn marriage; he is as consciously *wicked* as any illicit lover of romance and he consents to be damned for a personal devotion, never questioning the justice of the punishment he has incurred.

Huckleberry Finn was once barred from certain libraries and schools for its alleged subversion of morality. The authorities had in mind the book's endemic lying, the petty thefts, the denigrations of respectability and religion, the bad language, and the bad grammar. We smile at that excessive care, yet in point of fact *Huckleberry Finn* is indeed a subversive book—no one who reads thoughtfully the dialectic of Huck's great moral crisis will ever again be wholly able to accept without some question and some irony the assumptions of the respectable morality by which he lives, nor will ever again be certain that what he considers the clear dictates of moral reason are not merely the engrained customary beliefs of his time and place.

—Lionel Trilling, *"Huckleberry Finn," The Liberal Imagination: Essays on Literature and Society* (New York: Viking Press, 1950), pp. 110–13

LEO MARX ON THE ENDING OF *HUCKLEBERRY FINN*

[Leo Marx (b. 1919) is a leading American critic and author of *The Machine in the Garden: Technology and the Pastoral Ideal* (1964) and *The Pilot and the Passenger: Essays on Literature, Technology, and Culture in the United States* (1988). In this extract, Marx expresses the views of many critics in being dissatisfied with the seemingly contrived ending of the

novel, in which Jim had already been declared free by
his former owner, Miss Watson.]

I believe that the ending of *Huckleberry Finn* makes so many
readers uneasy because they rightly sense that it jeopardizes
the significance of the entire novel. To take seriously what happens at the Phelps farm is to take lightly the entire downstream
journey. What is the meaning of the journey? With this question all discussion of *Huckleberry Finn* must begin. It is true that
the voyage down the river has many aspects of a boy's idyl.
We owe much of its hold upon our imagination to the enchant-
ing image of the raft's unhurried drift with the current. The
leisure, the absence of constraint, the beauty of the river—all
these things delight us. "It's lovely to live on a raft." And the
multitudinous life of the great valley we see through Huck's
eyes has a fascination of its own. Then, of course, there is
humor—laughter so spontaneous, so free of the bitterness
present almost everywhere in American humor that readers
often forget how grim a spectacle of human existence Huck
contemplates. Humor in this novel flows from a bright joy of
life as remote from our world as living on a raft.

Yet along with the idyllic and the epical and the funny in
Huckleberry Finn, there is a coil of meaning which does for the
disparate elements of the novel what a spring does for a watch.
The meaning is not in the least obscure. It is made explicit
again and again. The very words with which Clemens launches
Huck and Jim upon their voyage indicate that theirs is not a
boy's lark but a quest for freedom. From the electrifying
moment when Huck comes back to Jackson's Island and rouses
Jim with the news that a search party is on the way, we are
meant to believe that Huck is enlisted in the cause of freedom.
"Git up and hump yourself, Jim!" he cries. "There ain't a minute
to lose. They're after us!" What particularly counts here is the
us. No one is after Huck; no one but Jim knows he is alive. In
that small word Clemens compresses the exhilarating power of
Huck's instinctive humanity. His unpremeditated identification
with Jim's flight from slavery is an unforgettable moment in
American experience, and it may be said at once that any cul-
mination of the journey which detracts from the urgency and
dignity with which it begins will necessarily be unsatisfactory.

Huck realizes this himself, and says so when, much later, he comes back to the raft after discovering that the Duke and the King have sold Jim:

> After all this long journey . . . here it was all come to nothing, everything all busted up and ruined, because they could have the heart to serve Jim such a trick as that, and make him a slave again all his life, and amongst strangers, too, for forty dirty dollars.

Huck knows that the journey will have been a failure unless it takes Jim to freedom. It is true that we do discover, in the end, that Jim is free, but we also find out that the journey was not the means by which he finally reached freedom.

The most obvious thing wrong with the ending, then, is the flimsy contrivance by which Clemens frees Jim. In the end we not only discover that Jim has been a free man for two months, but that his freedom has been granted by old Miss Watson. If this were only a mechanical device for terminating the action, it might not call for much comment. But it is more than that: it is a significant clue to the import of the last ten chapters. Remember who Miss Watson is. She is the Widow's sister whom Huck introduces in the first pages of the novel. It is she who keeps "pecking" at Huck, who tries to teach him to spell and to pray and to keep his feet off the furniture. She is an ardent proselytizer for piety and good manners, and her greed provides the occasion for the journey in the first place. She is Jim's owner, and he decides to flee only when he realizes that she is about to break her word (she cannot resist a slave trader's offer of eight hundred dollars) and sell him down the river away from his family.

Miss Watson, in short, is the Enemy. If we accept a predilection for physical violence, she exhibits all the outstanding traits of the valley society. She pronounces the polite lies of civilization that suffocate Huck's spirit. The freedom which Jim seeks, and which Huck and Jim temporarily enjoy aboard the raft, is accordingly freedom *from* everything for which Miss Watson stands. Indeed, the very intensity of the novel derives from the discordance between the aspirations of the fugitives and the respectable code for which she is a spokesman. Therefore, her regeneration, of which the deathbed freeing of Jim is the unconvincing sign, hints a resolution of the novel's essential conflict. Perhaps because this device most transparently reveals that shift in point of view which he could not avoid, and which is less easily discerned elsewhere in the concluding chapters, Clemens plays it down. He makes little attempt to account for Miss Watson's change of heart, a change particularly surprising in view of Jim's brazen escape. Had Clemens given this episode dramatic emphasis appropriate to its function, Miss Watson's bestowal of freedom upon Jim would have proclaimed what the rest of the ending actually accomplishes—a vindication of persons and attitudes Huck and Jim had symbolically repudiated when they set forth downstream.

—Leo Marx, "Mr. Eliot, Mr. Trilling, and *Huckleberry Finn*," *American Scholar* 22, No. 4 (Autumn 1953): 425–27

RALPH ELLISON ON HUCK AND JIM

[Ralph Ellison (1914–1994), an important black American novelist and author of *Invisible Man* (1952), also wrote a small body of literary criticism. In this extract, Ellison shows that Huck Finn regarded Jim as a genuine human being, and that his attempt to free Jim reveals Huck's simultaneous longing to be a part of society and his individualistic wish to escape it.]

Huckleberry Finn knew, as did Mark Twain, that Jim was not only a slave but a human being, a man who in some ways was to be envied, and who expressed his essential humanity in his desire for freedom, his will to possess his own labor, in his loyalty and capacity for friendship and in his love for his wife and child. Yet Twain, though guilty of the sentimentality common to humorists, does not idealize the slave. Jim is drawn in all his ignorance and superstition, with his good traits and his bad. He, like all men, is ambiguous, limited in circumstance but not in possibility. And it will be noted that when Huck makes his decision he identifies himself with Jim and accepts the judgment of his superego—that internalized representative of the community—that his action is evil. Like Prometheus, who for mankind stole fire from the gods, he embraces the evil implicit in his act in order to affirm his belief in humanity. Jim, therefore, is not simply a slave, he is a symbol of humanity, and in freeing Jim, Huck makes a bid to free himself of the conventionalized evil taken for civilization by the town.

This conception of the Negro as a symbol of Man—the reversal of what he represents in most contemporary thought—was organic to nineteenth-century literature. It occurs not only in Twain but in Emerson, Thoreau, Whitman and Melville (whose symbol of evil, incidentally, was white), all of whom were men publicly involved in various forms of deeply personal rebellion. And while the Negro and the color black were associated with the concept of evil and ugliness far back in the Christian era, the Negro's emergence as a symbol of value came, I believe, with Rationalism and the rise of the romantic individual of the eighteenth century. This, perhaps, because the romantic was in revolt against the old moral authority, and if he suffered a sense of guilt, his passion for personal freedom was such that he was willing to accept evil (a tragic attitude) even to identifying himself with the "noble slave"—who symbolized the darker, unknown potential side of his personality, that underground side, turgid with possibility, which might, if given a chance, toss a fistful of mud into the sky and create a "shining star."

Even that prototype of the bourgeois, Robinson Crusoe, stopped to speculate as to his slave's humanity. And the rising American industrialists of the late nineteenth century were to rediscover what their European counterparts had learned a century before: that the good man Friday was as sound an investment for Crusoe morally as he was economically, for not only did Friday allow Crusoe to achieve himself by working for him, but by functioning as a living scapegoat to contain Crusoe's guilt over breaking with the institutions and authority of the past, he made it possible to exploit even his guilt economically. The man was one of the first missionaries.

Mark Twain was alive to this irony and refused such an easy (and dangerous) way out. Huck Finn's acceptance of the evil implicit in his "emancipation" of Jim represents Twain's acceptance of his personal responsibility in the condition of society. This was the tragic fate behind his comic mask.

But by the twentieth century this attitude of tragic responsibility had disappeared from our literature along with that broad conception of democracy which vitalized the work of our greatest writers. After Twain's compelling image of black and white fraternity the Negro generally disappears from fiction as a rounded human being. And if already in Twain's time a novel which was optimistic concerning a democracy which would include all men could not escape being banned from public libraries, by our day his great drama of interracial fraternity had become, for most Americans at least, an amusing boy's story and nothing more. But, while a boy, Huck Finn has become by the somersault motion of what William Empson terms "pastoral," an embodiment of the heroic, and an exponent of humanism. Indeed, the historical and artistic justification for his adolescence lies in the fact that Twain was depicting a transitional period of American life; its artistic justification is that adolescence is the time of the "great confusion" during which both individuals and nations flounder between accepting and rejecting the responsibilities of adulthood. Accordingly, Huck's relationship to Jim, the river, and all they symbolize, is that of a humanist; in his relation to the community he is an individualist. He embodies the two major conflicting drives operating in nineteenth-century America. And if humanism is man's basic attitude toward a social order which he accepts, and individualism his basic attitude toward one he rejects, one might say that Twain, by allowing these two attitudes to argue dialectically in his work of art, was as highly moral an artist as he was a believer in democracy, and vice versa.

—Ralph Ellison, "Twentieth-Century Fiction and the Black Mask of Humanity" (1953), Shadow and Act (New York: Random House, 1964), pp. 31–34

LESLIE A. FIEDLER ON HUCK FINN AS THE "GOOD BAD BOY"

[Leslie A. Fiedler (b. 1917), the Samuel L. Clemens Professor of Literature at the State University of New York at Buffalo, is a leading American literary critic and advocate of the literary and cultural significance of popular literature. Among his many books are *Waiting for the End* (1964), *The Return of the Vanishing American* (1968), *Collected Essays* (1971), and *What Was Literature? Class Culture and Mass Society* (1982). Fiedler also wrote a famous essay, "Come Back to the Raft Ag'in, Huck Honey!" (1948), on the possible homoerotic overtones of *Huckleberry Finn.* In this extract, from his pioneering study, *Love and Death in the American Novel* (1960), Fiedler studies how Huck is a "good bad boy" in being both mischievous and at the same time morally upright.]

The Good Bad Boy is, of course, America's vision of itself, crude and unruly in his beginnings, but endowed by his creator with an instinctive sense of what is right. Sexually as pure as any milky maiden, he is a roughneck all the same, at once potent and submissive, made to be reformed by the right woman. No wonder our greatest book is about a boy and that boy "bad"! The book is, of course, *Huckleberry Finn* (with its extension back into *Tom Sawyer*), an astonishingly complicated novel, containing not one image of the boy but a series of interlocking ones. Tom Sawyer exists as the projection of all that Sid Sawyer, pious Good Good Boy, presumably yearns for and denies; but Huck Finn in turn stands for what Tom is not quite rebel enough to represent; and Nigger Jim (remade from boy to adult between the two books) embodies a world of instinct and primal terror beyond what even the outcast white boy projects.

In our national imagination, two freckle-faced boys, arm in arm, fishing poles over their shoulders, walk toward the river; or one alone floats peacefully on its waters, a runaway Negro by his side. They are on the lam, we know, from Aunt Polly and Aunt Sally and the widow Douglas and Miss Watson, from golden-haired Becky Thatcher, too—from all the reduplicated female symbols of "sivilization." It is these images of boyhood which the popular imagination further debases step by step via Penrod and Sam or O. Henry's "Red Chief" to Henry Aldrich on the radio or the insufferable Archie of the teen-age comic books. Such figures become constantly more false in their naïveté, in their hostility to culture in general and schoolteachers in particular; and it scarcely matters whether they are kept in the traditional costume of overalls or are permitted jeans and sweaters decorated with high-school letters.

Twain is surely not responsible for all the vulgar metamorphoses of his images of boyhood; but in one respect he is a conscious accomplice of the genteel kidnapers of Huck and Jim. Since not only in his avowed children's books, but almost everywhere in his work, Twain writes as a boy for a world accustomed to regarding the relations of the sexes in terms of the tie that binds mother to son. Not only does he disavow physical passion, refusing the Don Juan role traditional for European writers; but he downgrades even the Faustian role incumbent on American authors. In him, the diabolic outcast becomes the "little devil," not only comical but cute, a child who will outgrow his mischief, or an imperfect adult male, who needs the "dusting off" of marriage to a good woman. It was in the fading '60's that Twain's typical fictional devices were contrived, in the '70's that they were perfected—at a time, that is to say, when everywhere in the popular American novel the archetypes were being reduced to juveniles. As Clarissa becomes a small girl in *The Wide, Wide World,* so Werther becomes a child in Twain's total work, turns into the boy-author Mark Twain; and not only the American women who made Susan Warner's book a best-seller approve, but their husbands, too, who laughed at their wives' taste—just as Twain had at his wife's before being challenged to write *The Gilded Age.* Even dirty, tired, adult Europe approves, finds no offense in *The Innocents Abroad* itself, since Twain was playing a role that European self-hatred and condescension to the United States demanded, acting the Good Bad Boy of Western culture. For everyone, male and female, European and American, he represents the id subverting tired ego-ideals, not in terror and anarchy, but in horseplay, pranks, and irreverent jests.

—Leslie A. Fiedler, *Love and Death in the American Novel* (New York: Criterion Books, 1960; rev. ed. New York: Stein & Day, 1966), pp. 270–72

❖

A. E. Dyson on the Irony of Huck Finn's View of Society

[A. E. Dyson (b. 1928) is a distinguished British critic and author of *The Crazy Fabric: Essays in Irony* (1965) and, with Julian Lovelock, *Masterful Images: English Poetry from Metaphysicals to Romantics* (1976). He is a former Senior Lecturer in English and American Studies at the University of East Anglia. In this extract, Dyson shows how Huck Finn's view of himself in regard to his society is full of ironies, so that he ends up being a radical in spite of himself.]

How far is *Huckleberry Finn* the expression of a clear preference, either for radicalism or for the noble savage? The answer is not clear-cut. If one tries Mark Twain out with some radical causes of the present day, he can sometimes seem reactionary. He would have been anti-apartheid, of course; if his irony is committed to any obvious 'cause' it is that. But he might well have been for hanging rather than against it, on the familiar grounds, abundantly clear in his work, that reformers interested only in kindness overlooked the grim realities of human evil, against which society must protect itself strongly, even ruthlessly, to survive. Huck's charity, it is true, transcends this, by way of an equally ruthless honesty on the other side. Confronted with the murderers trapped on the boat, he reflects: 'I began to think how dreadful it was, even for murderers, to be in such a fix. I says to myself, there ain't no telling but I might come to be a murderer myself, yet, and then how would I like it?' And when the Duke and the King have perpetrated every possible treachery against both himself and Jim, he can still spare them compassion in their own misery and suffering. But Mark Twain himself, on the whole, feels that murderers and others like them deserve what they get; as to the do-gooders like the new judge who thinks he can reform Huck's father by kindness, they come in for frequent satiric treatment at his hands.

Mark Twain takes evil seriously, in other words, and he believes that strong social law is necessary to combat it, even though law will be tainted with the defects of the class who make it. This becomes more obvious when one thinks of the really anti-social figures in *Huckleberry Finn*. Huck's father, the Duke and the King are all failures, who stand outside society not because they are too honest for it, like Huck, or unjustly discriminated against by it, like Jim, but simply because they are lazy, vicious, and by nature parasitic. The passage in which Huck's father fulminates against the Government for tolerating an educated 'nigger' is irony of the straightforwardly boomerang kind, and of him, as of the other scoundrels in the book, there is no good word to be said. Though Huck understands and pities them, and sees himself partly in the same boat, he certainly does not approve of them, and he is nothing like them himself. In an important sense, they represent what happens when the respectable virtues are rejected outright—the good like duty, justice, responsibility along with the bad—and for Twain the last state is clearly worse than the first.

Huck himself, and to a great extent Jim, are wholly different from this. They represent not the rejection of society's highest values, but their fulfilment. The irony here is that society rejects Huck for being too good; by living up to his own ideals he becomes unfamiliar, and offers a challenge which can easily be mistaken for something stupid, or sceptical, or subversive. On the raft, Huck and Jim become what Lionel Trilling has called a 'community of saints'; yet their values come not from the civilised society which is supposed to encourage saints, but from the older incentive of a common danger, a common humanity, a common predicament.

It is here that the most penetrating ironic effects take place. The fact that Huck thinks himself worse, rather than better, than his fellows leads to the major irony that from first to last he sees the help he gives Jim as a sin; and the notion of selling Jim back into bondage can repeatedly present itself as a prompting to repentance and virtue. There are the harrowing moments when he wavers; and the final victory when he says 'All right, I'll go to Hell then' is all the more powerful for being unrecognised by Huck himself as savouring of either paradox or irony.

Nor should one underestimate the nature of Huck's stand at this moment. A large part of the country's economy depended on slavery, and one knows for a fact that even tender consciences have difficulty in seeing very clearly when this is so. Again and again the point is underlined. The question is asked, 'Anyone hurt?', and Huck answers, quite naturally, 'No mum; one nigger killed.' The doctor towards the end of the tale assumes that recapturing a runaway slave is a more pressing moral duty than attending to a patient. Huck himself is horrified to think that Tom Sawyer might have degenerated into a 'nigger stealer', and is relieved to discover that this is not so. All of this may be slightly exaggerated for purposes of the irony, but truth can sometimes defy a satirist to improve upon it for his purpose. The depth to which an economic condition causes moral blindness is deeper, at any rate, than Huck's conscious moralising can reach. Huck really thinks he *is* being wicked, and the irony here cuts straight from writer to reader, bypassing Huck himself, though enhancing his stature.

One can see, from this central point, what Mark Twain is really doing. Though he rejects ideals that strike him as facile or dangerous, he holds passionately to the conviction that underlies all true radical feeling: namely, that all men should be treated as equally human, irrespective of the natural or manmade barriers of colour, class, belief or what you will. That men are not equally good he acknowledges, and that some are too bad to be tolerated he also admits. But that a man should be despised simply for being brought up in poverty, like Huck, or for being the wrong colour, like Jim, fills him with outrage. In presenting the pair of them as the salt of the earth he is making a most profoundly radical point. He is also doing more. The decency of Huck and Jim offers some hope for the human species itself: an original virtue, perhaps, constantly departed from, and paradoxically exiled, yet ultimately not to be eradicated from the human heart.

—A. E. Dyson, "Mark Twain, *Huckleberry Finn* and the Whole Truth," *The Crazy Fabric: Essays in Irony* (London: Macmillan, 1965), pp. 106–8

[James M. Cox (b. 1925) is a former Avalon Professor of Humanities at Dartmouth College and author of *Recovering Literature's Lost Ground* (1989). In this extract, taken from *Mark Twain: The Fate of Humor* (1962), Cox discusses Mark Twain's use of the vernacular dialect for Huck Finn's first-person narration of his story, showing that Twain transforms dialect from merely a means for humor or parody into a means for the exploration of character.]

To say that in *Huckleberry Finn* Mark Twain extended his humor into serious territory is not to say that his humor became serious, but that larger areas of seriousness came under the dominion of his humor. If the turning of serious issues into the form of humor was the substantial inversion of the book, the formal inversion lay in transforming dialect into vernacular, which is to say making it the vehicle of vision. In terms of literary history, *Huckleberry Finn* marks the full emergence of an American language, and although Mark Twain did not accomplish the process alone, he *realized* the tradition which he inherited. The "Southwest" humorists—Hooper, Longstreet, Harris and Thorpe; the comic journalists—Artemus Ward, Petroleum V. Nasby, Josh Billings, and John Phoenix; and the local colorists—Harriet Beecher Stowe, Bret Harte, Mary E. Wilkins Freeman, and Sarah Orne Jewett—had all used dialect. Yet in the humor of the old Southwest and in the literary achievements of the local colorists, the dialect was framed by a literary language which invariably condescended to it. The comic journalists, though they dropped the literary frame to appear as "characters," reduced dialect to a comic image. If the Southwest humorists tended to brutalize dialect characters and local colorists to sentimentalize them, the comic journalists, by reducing themselves to dialect, sought to give pungency and quaintness to conventional thought.

But something altogether different happens in *Huckleberry Finn*. The language is neither imprisoned in a frame nor distorted into a caricature; rather, it becomes a way of casting character and experience at the same time. This combination is the fine economy of Huckleberry Finn's style. Thus when Huck declares at the outset that he, not Mark Twain, will write this book, the language at one and the same time defines character and action.

> You don't know about me without you have read a book by the name *The Adventures of Tom Sawyer*; but that ain't no matter. That book was made by Mr. Mark Twain, and he told the truth, mainly. There was things which he stretched, but mainly he told the truth. That is nothing. I never see anybody but lied one time or another, without it was Aunt Polly, or the Widow, or maybe Mary. Aunt Polly—Tom's Aunt Polly, she is—and Mary, and the Widow Douglas is all told about in that book, which is mostly a true book, with some stretchers, as I said before.

Nothing more seems to be going on here than in previous uses of dialect. But by allowing Huck's vernacular merely to *imply* the literary form, Mark Twain was reorganizing the entire value system of language, for all values had to be transmitted directly or indirectly through Huck's vernacular. In turning the narration over to Huck, Mark Twain abandoned the explicit norms and risked making his vernacular force the reader to supply the implied norms. The vernacular he developed created the means of control within the reader's mind, chiefly in three ways. First of all, Huck's incorrect language implied standard, correct, literary English. Second, Huck's status as a child invited an indulgence from the reader. Finally, Huck's action in time and place—freeing a slave in the Old South before the Civil War—insured moral approval from the reader. Though he is being a bad boy in his own time, he is being a good boy in the reader's imagination.

All these controls, which are really *conventions*, exist outside the novel. They are just what the style of the novel is *not*; for the style is the inversion which implies the conventions yet remains their opposite. And this style is Mark Twain's revolution in language, his rebellion in form; and it marks the emergence of the American language to which both Hemingway and Faulkner allude when they say that Mark Twain was the first American writer, the writer from whom they descend.

—James M. Cox, *Mark Twain: The Fate of Humor* (Princeton: Princeton University Press, 1966), pp. 167–69

[George C. Carrington, Jr. (1928–1990) was for many
years a professor of English at Northern Illinois
University. He was the author of several books on
Twain's contemporary William Dean Howells. In this
extract, taken from his book, *The Dramatic Unity of*
Huckleberry Finn (1976), Carrington places Twain's
novel in the history of the period, showing how Huck
Finn's attitude toward slaves is a mirror of the complex
and paradoxical attitudes of the people of his time—
and ours.]

By the late 1870s and early 1880s, when Twain was working
on *Huckleberry Finn*, he had grown beyond the mechanical
topical novel and was working with a complex mixture of local
color, southwestern humor, nostalgia, and myth; yet he was so
completely of his era and his culture that when he stumbled
into treating the extended relationship of a black slave and a
white youth, at the very time (1876–83) that the nation was
undergoing a fundamental shift in its relation to blacks, he
could not help paralleling the national drama-sequence. In
chapter 31 Huck would sincerely "go to hell" to free Jim; a few
hours later he is thrown off stride by the situation at the
Phelpses; a few hours after that he is easily seduced by Tom
Sawyer into a grandiose scheme that uses the rescue of Jim as
a means to an end; eventually Huck loses all but a spectator's
interest in Jim. Rather like a group of genteel Hucks, the northern middle class, many of them former Radical Republicans
who had fought to free the slaves, became irritated by the long
bother of Reconstruction, became tired of southern hostility,
and were easily seduced by strong-willed politicians and busi-
nessmen into abandoning the freedmen for new excitements
like railroad building. In the crucial event, the Compromise of
1877, the Republican leaders traded withdrawal of the last
troops from the South in return for the electoral votes of three
southern states and continued control of the federal government. The spirit that led the country to accept the Compromise
might ironically be called "the spirit of '77." Absorbed in his
work and his new life in Hartford, Twain shared that spirit. He

thought the Compromise a very good thing indeed. Three generations later the white civil-rights movement of the 1960s took a similar course: enthusiasm and dedication followed by loss of interest and absorption in new issues. "The spirit of '77" is still in us.

Adventures of Huckleberry Finn is thus not only a great but a sadly typical American drama of race: not a stark tragedy of black suffering, but a complex tragicomedy of white weakness and indifference. It is one of those modern books that, as Lionel Trilling says, "read us," tell "us," Trilling's well-meaning, confused liberal Americans, about ourselves. In *Huckleberry Finn* Twain obeys Thoreau's basic rule, followed in many American masterworks, "to drive life into a corner, and reduce it to its lowest terms, and, if it proved to be mean, why then to get the whole and genuine meanness of it, and publish its meanness to the world." The meanness of *Huckleberry Finn* is not that man is evil but that he is weak and doomed to remain weak. This vision of man is embarrassing at best and unbearable at worst. As Stanley Elkins says of slavery, "There is a painful touchiness in all aspects of the subject; the discourse contains almost too much immediacy, it makes too many connections with present problems." Twain did not shirk the presentation, but managed to avert his gaze from the subject's Medusa horrors by looking at it through his uncomprehending narrator.

—George C. Carrington, Jr., The Dramatic Unity of Huckleberry
Finn (Columbus: Ohio State University Press, 1976), pp. 190–91

LOUIS J. BUDD ON THE CONTEMPORARY RESPONSE TO *HUCKLEBERRY FINN*

[Louis J. Budd (b. 1921) is one of the leading authorities on Mark Twain, being the author of *Mark Twain: Social Philosopher* (1971) and editor of *Critical Essays on Mark Twain* (1982–83; 2 vols.) and *New Essays on* Adventures of Huckleberry Finn (1985). He is a former professor of English at Duke University. In this extract, taken from his study, *Our Mark Twain: The Making of His Public Personality* (1983), Budd studies the response to Twain's novel both by the general public and by Twain himself, showing how the work confirmed Twain's reputation both as a humorist and as a political and moral radical.]

Ordinary readers, who stay refreshingly defiant of cultural traffic cops, liked *Huckleberry Finn* from the first. It serves up a feast of routines by a veteran newspaper humorist—farce, puns, comic misspellings, and parody of highbrow tastes. Currently a rage, local color also boosted the book, as did its genre painting or passages of kitchen realism. Besides the then rare pleasure of finding genuine vernacular in print, many savored its folksy touches sometimes entwined with bits of forgotten lore. These elements did not undercut Twain as go-getter; the era liked to think that its leaders and heroes were rooted in the village past. Any novel that lasts has also stirred the bone-deep appeals of narrative, starting with plot, and *Huckleberry Finn* keeps on the move with surprises and a changing cast. It can reasonably be called "lowbrow 'escape' fiction," a "pleasing and familiar package" in its "western locale, the picaresque adventures of its raffish characters, and the strongly subversive stance of its vagabond hero." Unanalytic conservatives can accept rebellion when it is properly hedged, as with pathos, and even enjoy irreverence when brandished by an expert tactician like Twain. Whether or not readers approved, they got a strong reminder of his earthiness, his insistence on chuckling over seedy rascals like the King and the Duke. He went on again to grin at the putrefactions of the flesh: Pap's "tree-toad white" skin, Jim as a Sick Arab, Huck's brains oozing out from under his hat, and the funeral "orgies" for Peter Wilks particularly offensive to one reviewer. At the other pole a few readers—joined by more each year—respected the author for his humaneness verging on profundity or—in our time—pessimism about oppression, conformity, and other social evils.

Beyond the conflicting signals *Huckleberry Finn* surely had a composite effect in 1885. It strengthened the impression of

Twain's energy that, along with his highly visible personal, civic, and business activities, he could produce so good another book so soon. Excerpted in three issues of the *Century*, it assured the magazine public of his rising status while the surprisingly wide newspaper debate over the banning in Concord underlined his controversiality as well as his importance. The author behind Huck clearly had a heart quick to despise pretense, an eye quicker to spot it in gesture or dress, and an ear tuned to register devastatingly the gamut of platitude, whether delivered in flossy English or vernacular. A free spirit, he was sometimes willfully playful but usually left a sting of satire. He had a passion for honesty with oneself, and his robustness of mind led to pragmatic ideals judged as closely as Sunday-school morals. Politically committed he sympathized with the freedmen and, more generally, with egalitarian self-respect. He was firmly true to his native, American origins rather than imported literary standards. For all his principles or his contempt toward pettiness, he rang to the core with warm humor and, of course, a genius for comedy at many levels, racing up and down them with reckless agility. Still, a personage of rich experience, he convincingly managed to sound informed on serious matters. So deceptively offhand in his skill at penetrating the surface of manners that the victim could topple before feeling the thrust, almost threatening in the freshness of his perceptions, impulsively kind while skeptical about the run of people, the author of *Huckleberry Finn* was a man on whom practically nothing was lost and yet who must be engagingly if fallibly human.

Twain was surprisingly slow to name *Huckleberry Finn* as his favorite book, often seeming to go along with the expected answer when he did so. If, as he plausibly claimed years later, he got "letters of sympathy and indignation . . . mainly from children" when the Concord Public Library banned it, he did not as yet realize that his junior corps of defenders had gained many permanent enlistees. Before deciding on publication he had fought spells of uncertainty, symbolized by the "heliotype" of a sculptured bust of himself pasted opposite the frontispiece drawing of Huck. Judging from the hundreds of photographs we now have, he faced the camera like a witness under oath, and he posed for the always more frequent oil portraits with the gravity of a banker or statesman or aristocrat. In 1887 he purged a woodcut of himself from the *Library of American Literature* being prepared for his firm: "The more I think of the gratuitous affront of wood where steel is lavished upon the unread & the forgotten, the more my bile rises." So we must speculate why, just as *Huckleberry Finn* was ready for typesetting, he incurred the expense and bother of adding the heliotype of his severely dignified bust even if it held up the "canvassing" copies. He explained tersely: "I thought maybe it would advantage the book." Certainly it could remind subscribers that the author behind the barely literate boy had demonstrable status in the up-to-date world and could write in a style to match it when needed. If they should ask about the sculptor, whom Twain had supported for years of study in France, that would work to the advantage of both.

> —Louis J. Budd, *Our Mark Twain: The Making of His Public Personality* (Philadelphia: University of Pennsylvania Press, 1983), pp. 89–91

Neil Schmitz on Huck Finn and His Raft

[Neil Schmitz is a professor of English at the State University of New York at Buffalo. He is the author of many critical essays. In this extract, Schmitz discusses Huck Finn's life on his raft, showing that this is where Huck learns most about himself and about the life around him.]

The actual raft is a modest affair: "a little section of a lumber raft—nice pine planks." Always specific, Huck gives us its exact size. "It was twelve foot wide and about fifteen or sixteen foot long, and the top stood above water six or seven inches, a solid level floor." Jim builds a "snug wigwam" on the raft, and raises the level of its floor "a foot or more above the level of the raft, so now the blankets and all the traps was out of reach of steamboat waves." Inside the wigwam "we made a layer of dirt about five or six inches deep with a frame around it for to hold it to its place; this was to build a fire on in sloppy weather or chilly; the wigwam would keep it from being seen." So the found raft, a mere floor, becomes a dwelling-place raised above the water, a home with a roof and a hearth, the completion of fire. Having lived in a barrel, in the cleanliness of the Widow's house, in the squalor of Pap's cabin, in a makeshift tent on Jackson's Island, and then in a cave, Huck at last finds the peace and freedom of a dwelling-place. And the food is excellent: fish, bacon, meal, a filched chicken now and then, watermelon, mushmelon, fresh corn. The luxuries Huck and Jim add by scavenging are perfect for the contemplative nature of raft life: three boxes of "prime" seegars, a small batch of books, and a spyglass. In their abode, snug, warm, and dry, they can still feel closely beneath them, a few feet away, the large motion of the "big still river." They travel at night. A watchlight is hung to warn off steamboats. "It was kind of solemn, drifting down the big still river, laying on our backs looking up at the stars, and we didn't ever feel like talking loud, and it warn't often that we laughed, only a little kind of a low chuckle." Such is the meaningful raft Huck constructs in his narrative, plank by plank. It is the place where he dwells, where he is most present, most himself, Huck's Huck. Here for the first time he feels the rapture of intimacy, the highest meaning of dwelling, and this is the beam that holds the raft together for Huck, that makes it resemble (for us) the marriage bed Ishmael and Queequeg fraternally share in *Moby-Dick*. Huck gives us in exact detail the thingness of the raft, its dimension, its equipment, the feel of it, but all this ardent phenomenology ultimately depends on Jim's presence. What the raft means to Huck is not the meaning of the raft in *Huckleberry Finn*.

Indeed Huck's dwelling, this "snug" home, has no foundation, is not grounded. It is rather given over to the "big still river" that runs "over four mile an hour." The river sends Huck the raft and sustains Huck's life on the raft, but the river is also serial time and linear direction, history and geography. It is a relation Huck never seems to understand completely, that position on the river (above Cairo, below Cairo) determines the significance of the raft. "Take it all around," he recalls in Chapter 12, "we lived pretty high." And again in Chapter 18, writing of the resurrected raft, the post-Cairo raft, the doomed raft, Huck declares his devotion: "You feel mighty free and easy and comfortable on a raft." For Jim, who never joins Huck in these rhapsodies, the raft has meaning *only* in relation to the river. On Jackson's Island, before the actual raft appears, he has already tactically concluded that a raft is the safest way to make his crossing: "ef I stole a skift to cross over, dey'd miss dat skift, you see, en dey'd know 'bout whah I'd lan' on de yuther side en whah to pick up my track. So I says, a raff is what I's arter; it doan' *make* no track." Above Cairo, then, the raft is simply a ferry he has fixed up with Huck's help, an opportune mode of transport. His gaze is directed elsewhere, at the muddy expanse of the Mississippi, which he anxiously scans, looking for the "big clear river" that will signify the emptying of the Ohio, his destination, the point of his deliverance. Below Cairo the raft is briefly a refuge, a relief for Jim who has been hiding in a swamp, and then the stage on which he is at once humiliated and betrayed. The geographical river, the crucial river for Jim, effectively defines the nature and extent of his discourse on the raft. Approaching Cairo, Jim is increasingly contentious in his speech, self-assertive. After Cairo, absurdly floating down river, he lapses into poignant reveries, or is silent, out of Huck's story. "'Goodness sakes,'" asks Huck, and the question is telling, "'would a runaway nigger run *south?*'"

The essential drama of *Huckleberry Finn* therefore occurs on the raft. Huck's adventures on the shore are outlying, contingent, elaborative. He is always right in these episodes, afflicted innocence. On the raft Huck is wrong, Huck falls into contradiction, Huck grapples with the issue of his identity. Here he delivers his finest soliloquy. And there are other performers on this platform, other frames of reference, other speeches. The story Huck wants to tell is the story of a chase—"They're after us!"—and bring Jim as a sidekick into the play of that fiction. So he is always quick to draw upon that dubious pronoun, *we,* and he is proud of the getaway raft. It is finally a nifty little number, trim, with all the accessories. Yet the premise of Jim's tale is the axiom of a different genre in American literature, the beginning of each slave narrative: "I owns mysef." The question for Huck is the extent to which, at the risk of his own fiction, the pleasure of the raft, he will admit into recognition the contraposed existence of Jim's story—hear it, understand it, write it. It is as well the question of the style itself, the risk of *Huckleberry Finn* as a humorous text, whether humor can know suffering without denial or deception, without motive, moral or plot. Huck clings to his idea of the raft; it is the only thing he can properly call his own in *Huckleberry Finn,* the only place where he has a sense of humor, and he clings to his friendship with Jim, which is (for him) the guarantee of the raft's goodness, the assurance of its fun. On the shore Huck is always someone else, disguised, an observer. On the raft, with Jim, he is himself: naked, supple, finny. The two values, raft life and Jim, are incompatible.

> —Neil Schmitz, "Huckspeech," *Of Huck and Alice: Humorous Writing in American Literature* (Minneapolis: University of Minnesota Press, 1983), pp. 110–12

JAY MARTIN ON "DOUBLING" MOTIFS IN *HUCKLEBERRY FINN*

[Jay Martin (b. 1935), Leo S. Bing Professor of English and American Literature at the University of Southern California at Los Angeles, is the author of biographies of Conrad Aiken (1962), Nathanael West (1970), and Henry Miller (1978), and of *Who Am I This Time? Uncovering the Fictive Personality* (1988). In this extract, Martin studies how Twain has set up a variety of paired figures in his novel, including the most intriguing pair of all—himself and Huck Finn.]

Huckleberry Finn involves Huck not only in a series of parent-son situations but also in an equally potent succession of brotherly arrangements. Throughout his career, Twain took up the theme of the varied relations between two brothers—twins, doubles, intimate friends, older brother and younger, dandy and squatter, sophisticate and innocent, the powerful and the weak, Negro and white. From book to book, of course, he considered their relations in a variety of ways, but one basic plot feature that emerged early held on and became a fundamental feature of Twain's stories. He starts with two brothers, one apparently more powerful than the other. Then he reverses their positions. As a result, the weaker, younger, more innocent "brother" wins or gains a superior position. Finally, he returns to the original relation. Just as Sam had proclaimed his triumph concerning Henry's death by confessing his wishes, even as he condemned himself for them; so, in his literary work, he restored the "brothers" to their "proper" positions. In brief, the action of the novel shows the superior brother losing his position, changing places with the weaker, then, at last, regaining his original position. The psychological purpose of this pattern of power relations, considered from Twain's point of view, is clear. He identified with the older brother; he suffered punishment by losing his power; then, having expiated his guilt, he reassumed his position of power. This pattern of doubling, reversal, and release from guilt was not only a literary device but also a deeply personal response operating automatically in Twain's books and Twain's psyche.

Twain famously described the theme of *Huckleberry Finn* as the conflict between "A sound heart & a deformed conscience." The terms are of fundamental importance. In Huck's story, conscience suffers defeat. Twain was himself engaged in the same struggle to defeat his conscience and reveal his "sound heart." Huckleberry Finn is, as Twain doubtless wishes himself to be, an only child, without parents, without brothers. He is free from a guilt-ridden conscience and the influences of a Christian civilization in general. Yet, he gets subjected to various authorities, "fathers," or rule-givers, from the judge and Miss Watson and the Widow Douglas, to his own father, the Grangerfords, the King and the Duke, and finally Uncle Silas and Aunt Sally. He manages to escape from all of these and resume his own ways. At the same time, he gets associated with several "brothers"—with Tom Sawyer and the gang (they become "blood brothers"), with Jim, with Buck, and finally again with Tom Sawyer masquerading as Sid. Huck's doubling and reversal of roles, allied with an attack upon parental super-egos from which he escapes, gave Twain a chance, at least temporarily, to extricate himself through Huck from the guilty tangle that Sam Clemens had gotten him into.

In the very narrative form of the book itself Twain creates his own younger-older, weak-powerful, "unsivilized"-civilized, tale-telling twins: Huckleberry Finn and Mr. Mark Twain. The same pattern is evident here. As a professional novelist, Mr. Mark Twain is the older, stronger brother in the telling of tales. He has told *The Adventures of Tom Sawyer*. But the new novel begins as Huck seizes the story from him and in the process vindicates Mr. Twain from wrongdoing by assuring us that he had mainly told the truth. Still, Huck is bent on conveying a different level of truth. There is a considerable distance between the boy's tale and a conventional narrative by a professional novelist. The sort of narrative Huck tells opposes all accepted conventional narrative rules of novels. On the surface, it is full of defects—false starts, contradictions, mixed genres, and plot confusions. But Huck's tale turns out to be superior. Underneath, it has the "sound heart" of a true tale. Twain revealed his own sound artistic heart precisely by using his weaker novelistic brother, Huck, to destroy the surface order, the literary conscience and aesthetic appeal of the novel-narrative, and finally by going behind Huck's vernacular language to tell the truth—which he knew but could not speak—of his own heart.

> —Jay Martin, "The Genie in the Bottle: Huckleberry Finn in Mark Twain's Life," *One Hundred Years of* Huckleberry Finn: *The Boy, His Book, and American Culture,* ed. Robert Sattelmeyer and J. Donald Crowley (Columbia: University of Missouri Press, 1985), pp. 70–71

DAVID E. E. SLOANE ON THE DUKE AND THE DAUPHIN

[David E. E. Sloane (b. 1948) is the author of *Mark Twain as a Literary Comedian* (1973) and Sister Carrie, *Theodore Dreiser's Sociological Tragedy* (1992). He is a professor of English at the University of New Haven. In this extract, he studies the episode of the Duke and the Dauphin, showing how it is an encapsulation of many of the themes running through the entire novel.]

The Duke and Dauphin on entrance are unprepossessing even to Huck. Both are dressed "ornery," as Huck details their country clothes. Both are clearly small-time scoundrels preying on people more ignorant than themselves—one removing tartar from teeth but taking the enamel with it, the other doing good "business" as a temperance revivalist, but caught drinking and now on the run to escape being tarred and feathered. Preying on women and children is a particularly characteristic action for the pair, later expanded in the camp meeting and Wilks episodes. The first elaborates his "line" as patent-medicines, theater-acting, mesmerism, phrenology, singing school and geography, and "anything that comes handy, so it ain't work." The second, older man specializes in laying on of hands to cure cancer and paralysis, fortune-telling, and preaching at camp meetings and missionarying around, as he puts it: "Layin' on o' hands is my best holt." As with the slave-hunters, disease for others is a matter of indifference in comparison to money, but here it is more predatory. The men prey on pain and illness; their shiftiness and role-playing is not comparable to that of Huck and Jim. It takes advantage of and damages others for profit; it is more evil than the chameleon evasiveness of Huck and Jim. It is the most sinister adult form of the practices of . . . Tom Sawyer.

Immediately, as the two "beats" settle themselves on Huck and Jim's raft, the younger man takes to "alassin'" about his fate and both men announce themselves as banished royalty, establishing in the central action Twain's bête noir, monarchical authority. The mentality of absolutism can easily be treated in burlesque, since even in noncaricature, as in *The Prince and the Pauper,* much of the absurdity of royalty is shown either in egregious melodrama or in ironically described events and slapstick. To Twain open fraudulence claiming monarchal authority for personal gain is merely comic shorthand for historical fact.

Manipulating the language of cheap romances, against a counterpoint of skepticism from the old man, the young man reveals that he has been brought down from his rightful place as the Duke of Bridgewater. The Duke's revelation is false, but it makes Huck and Jim momentarily credulous, and they agree to solace him by calling him "Your Grace." The older man, angry, then takes hold of the false pretension to announce himself as the rightful heir to the throne of France, "in blue jeans and misery." The Dauphin counsels the now sulky Duke to accept his lower status, for he can still usurp the raft's ease—"plenty grub and an easy life." Royalty arrogates to itself the goods and earned wealth of the lower class; the Duke and king's acts are a microcosm of Twain's view of authoritarian power in government. Tom Sawyer will do likewise, rising to ever crazier heights of pretension in the "evasion."

Huck, as noted earlier, accommodates this reconciliation within the raft ethic. The Dauphin successfully cajoles the Duke, "It ain't my fault I warn't born a duke. . . . Make the best o' things the way you find 'em, says I." Huck and Jim, in turn, declare their gladness to see the handshaking reconciliation, and they expose their raft ethic now in subordination to a falsely imposed political power: "We felt mighty good over it, because it would a been a miserable business to have any unfriendliness on the raft, for what you want, above all things, on a raft, is for everybody to be satisfied, and feel right and kind towards the others." With this statement, Huck identifies the higher law of humanity (above all things) that has made his relationship with Jim a uniquely personal adventure. Here it becomes the property of the locus "raft." Now, we as readers truly understand that we have an independent and specially defined world, even as it succumbs to the vulnerability of all places in the world to control by the politically corrupt.

Huck also reveals his own insight, casting a strange and doubtful light over his failure to protect the raft in the first place. He comments that he knew that the liars were "lowdown humbugs and frauds." However, he keeps silent so as not to cause trouble, to "keep peace in the family"—a slanting reference to the P. T. Barnum Museum's "Happy Family" where the lamb and lion occupied the same cage. Olive Logan, a showwoman and platform lecturer influenced by Artemus Ward, had long before revealed, in *The Mimic World* (1871), that Barnum's effect was achieved by having the lion secretly drugged with morphine. Everything about this expression of ethics is thus problematical, and it becomes more so. Huck says, "If I never learnt nothing else out of pap, I learnt that the best way to get along with his kind of people is to let them have their own way." We recall that Huck could well have been murdered by his drunken Pap. Huck is thus in the most passive position possible for a free man; only his status as a boy allows for this philosophical passivity to be fictionally convincing. So Huck does not tell Jim and is willing to call the fake nobility by their titles. Such a philosophy almost assures us of the necessity for Huck's final decision at the end of the book to flee to "the Territories." Linked to Pap, the rapscallions are linked to, and imply a taint of, St. Petersburg.

The identification of the raft world is complete. The portion of the novel occupied by the Duke and the Dauphin—eleven of forty-three chapters—will now restate and expand the major themes of the novel. The indictment of religion is broadened negatively through the camp meeting sequence and positively through Mary Jane Wilks's endorsement of Huck. The vulgar venality of the American small town is elaborated through Bricksville and the Royal Nonesuch sequence. Separate from the minor swindles of the Duke and Dauphin, but within this framework, comes the indictment of lynch law, social order and religion, and human psychology presented in the Boggs-Sherburn and the circus episodes. The episode around the Wilks girls in which Huck foils the Duke and the Dauphin compensates the reader for the loss of the raft and Jim's freedom to Tom, but foreshadows the feeling that determines Huck's ultimate flight from civilization.

—David E. E. Sloane, Adventures of Huckleberry Finn: *American Comic Vision* (Boston: Twayne, 1988), pp. 87–89

BERNARD W. BELL ON TWAIN'S ATTITUDE TO JIM

[Bernard W. Bell is a professor of English at Pennsylvania State University and author of *The Afro-American Novel and Its Tradition* (1987). In this extract, taken from an anthology of essays by black scholars on *Huckleberry Finn,* Bell follows up on Ralph Ellison's

Does the historical and literary evidence support the notion that America's most popular and representative nineteenth-century humorist and satirist escaped or outgrew the influence of the racial prejudice and discrimination endemic to the period? Born and bred in the antebellum Southwest, a volunteer in the Confederate militia, and an advocate of the delightful accuracy of minstrelsy, Twain, as we will see, struggles valiantly, like Huck, to reject the legacy of American racism and to accept his personal share of responsibility for the injustice of slavery, but never in *Adventures of Huckleberry Finn* does he fully and unequivocally accept the equality of blacks. "Writing at a time when the blackfaced minstrel was still popular, and shortly after a war which left even the abolitionists weary of those problems associated with the Negro, Twain," as Ralph Ellison noted in the 1950s during the public attack by blacks on the racial offensiveness of the book, "fitted Jim into the outlines of the minstrel tradition, and it is from behind this stereotype mask that we see Jim's dignity and human capacity—and Twain's complexity—emerge." The portrayal of the complex humanity of Jim and Twain—the pernicious, tragic racism as well as the compassion behind their comic, occasionally ironic, masks—can best be fully understood and appreciated as an American classic rather than trash by interpreting *Adventures of Huckleberry Finn* in its sociohistorical as well as its literary context. ⟨. . .⟩

The ambiguity and ambivalence of Twain's relationship to Jim is vividly illustrated in chapter 15 when Jim violates the ethics of Jim Crow and noblesse oblige by reprimanding Huck for ridiculing him:

> When I got all wore out wid work, en wid de callin' for you, en went to sleep, my heart wuz mos' broke bekase you wuz los', en I didn' k'yer no mo' what become er me en de raf'. En when I wake up en fine you back agin, all safe en soun', de tears come en I could a got down on my knees en kiss' yo' foot I's so thankful. En all you wuz thinkin' 'bout wuz how you could make

a fool uv ole Jim wid a lie. Dat truck dah is *trash;* en trash is what people is dat puts dirt on de head er dey fren's en makes 'em ashamed.

Here Jim's deep moral indignation surfaces from behind the comic mask which he wears defensively to conceal his true feelings and thoughts from Huck and other whites who pervert their humanity in demeaning or denying his. (The mask slips again when he vows to free his wife and children even if he must steal them.) Huck, in response, feels so bad that he "could almost kissed *his* foot to get him to take it back. It was fifteen minutes before I could work myself up to go and humble myself to a nigger—but I done it and I warn't ever sorry for it afterwards, neither." Huck's contrition here and his subsequent resolve not merely to go to hell but to steal Jim out of slavery represent Twain's moral identification with both Jim and Huck. For Ellison, "Huck Finn's acceptance of the evil implicit in his 'emancipation' of Jim represents Twain's acceptance of his personal responsibility in the condition of society. This was the tragic face behind the comic mask." This perceptive interpretation certainly redeems narrative and author from being the trash that some would consign them to; for me and many other readers, though, Twain's tragic face is his failure of moral courage in reducing the complexity of Jim's assumption of manhood to a minstrel mask in the closing chapters. Jim's compromise of his desire for freedom, love of family, and self-respect in return for the forty dollars Tom gives him for cooperation in the burlesque escape plan is the tragic face behind his minstrel mask.

It is sad but true for many black readers that Twain's "Nigger" Jim is the best example of the humanity of black American slaves in nineteenth-century white American fiction. It is ironic, finally, as Ellison observed more than twenty-five years ago, that "down at the deep dark bottom of the melting pot, where the private is public and the public is private, where black is white and white is black, where the immoral becomes moral and the moral is anything that makes one feel good (or that one has the power to sustain), the white man's relish is apt to be the black man's gall." Having boasted to Andrew Lang of writing for the belly rather than the head of the white post-Reconstruction masses, Twain—nostalgically and metaphorically—sells Jim's soul down the river for laughs at the end of *Adventures of Huckleberry Finn*.

—Bernard W. Bell, "Twain's 'Nigger' Jim: The Tragic Face behind the Minstrel Mask," *Satire or Evasion? Black Perspectives on* Huckleberry Finn, ed. James S. Leonard, Thomas A. Tenney, and Thadious M. Davis (Durham, NC: Duke University Press, 1992), pp. 124–25, 137–38

HENRY B. WONHAM ON THE NARRATION OF *HUCKLEBERRY FINN*

[Henry B. Wonham is the author of *Mark Twain and the Art of the Tall Tale* (1993), from which this extract is taken. Here Wonham, studying the effects of Huck Finn narrating his own story, claims that this narrative strategy results not so much in overt humor as in irony: the reader must be constantly interpreting the deadpan language of Huck from a perspective different from that of Huck himself.]

As Huck points out on the first page of his narrative, *Huckleberry Finn* is not another deadpan performance by "Mr. Mark Twain," but an autobiographical account by a semiliterate boy who, had he known what trouble it would be to write a book, "wouldn't a tackled it" in the first place. Critics have made much of the transfer of narrative responsibility, with its liberating implications for Twain's style and imagination, but what actually occurs is less a revolutionary discovery in perspective than a subtle division of the formerly unified stage and literary persona. The "Mark Twain" who so impressed Noah Brooks and others operated by sustaining apparently contradictory attitudes within a single character, producing a sort of condensed version of the old Twain-Brown confrontation. That binary persona breaks down in *Huckleberry Finn* when the deadpan attitude ceases to function as a mere pose for the implied humorist and instead comes to life as something dynamic, creative, and independent. Huck combines the dubious attributes of the Simpleton, the Tenderfoot, and the Sufferer, and his grave seriousness makes him appear "innocently unaware" of the humor and hypocrisy his tale expresses. Like Mark Twain on stage, he is "anxious and perturbed"; he sometimes frames his sentences with a "painful effort"; he finds little to laugh at and much to worry about; in short, Huck's narration places a straight face over the occasionally comic, more often cruelly absurd, world of Mark Twain's Mississippi Valley. But the twin characteristics of the yarn-spinning persona, the grim demeanor and the smile it conceals, no longer belong to the same character. Huck, as the novel's grave expression, is a rhetorical posture made real. He does not qualify exactly as a yarn spinner himself, because he enjoys no access to the perspective of the implied humorist and because his solemn performance is never posed. He is a disembodied yarn spinner, the deadpan attitude come to life as part of a yarn-spinning strategy, often comically mistaken in his literal judgments and his grave outlook, but genuinely rather than affectedly ignorant of his mistakes.

Because Huck, unlike the deadpan poses of Twain's other writings, remains entirely cut off from the perspective of the implied humorist, Mark Twain as an authorial commentator remains equally cut off from Huck's narrative consciousness. ⟨John C.⟩ Gerber notes that Twain's best writing occurred when the pose placed limitations on the humorist—that is, when the demands of characterization forced Twain "to make his satire implicit" and to "avoid authorial underlining." On stage and in the writings narrated by versions of the stage persona, Twain's satire tended to be heavy-handed, if not explicit, for the humorist was never very far behind the solemn mask through which he spoke. With Huck in the role of deadpan narrator, however, satire and humorous commentary are forced farther beneath the surface. Huck articulates absurdities solemnly, in a manner befitting Simon Wheeler or Jim Baker of *A Tramp Abroad,* but Huck's seriousness operates comically only for the reader and his interpretive cohort, the implied humorist, whose powerful sense of irony places constant pressure on the reader's interpretive endeavor without penetrating or undermining the hero's conscious narration. As a result—and as Huck comments on the raft—laughter remains curiously outside the text, much as the humor of a tall tale emerges more from what cultural insiders are able to infer about the yarn spinner's performance than from the "text" of his performance itself.

—Henry B. Wonham, *Mark Twain and the Art of the Tall Tale* (New York: Oxford University Press, 1993), pp. 148–50

Books by
Mark Twain

The Celebrated Jumping Frog of Calaveras County and Other Sketches. 1867.

Address to His Imperial Majesty:—Alexander II. Emperor of Russia. 1867.

The Public to Mark Twain: Correspondence. 1868.

The Innocents Abroad; or, The New Pilgrims' Progress. 1869.

Mark Twain's (Burlesque) Autobiography and First Romance. 1871.

Mark Twain's Memoranda. 1871.

Roughing It. 1872.

The Innocents at Home. 1872.

A Curious Dream and Other Sketches. 1872.

Letter to the New York Tribune. 1873.

The Gilded Age: A Tale of To-day (with Charles Dudley Warner). 1873.

Sketches. 1874.

Speech on Accidental Insurance. 1874.

Sketches, New and Old. 1875.

The Adventures of Tom Sawyer. 1876.

Old Times on the Mississippi. 1876.

A True Story and The Recent Carnival of Crime. 1877.

An Idle Excursion. 1878.

Punch, Brothers, Punch! and Other Sketches. 1878.

Mark Twain on Babies. c. 1879.

A Tramp Abroad. 1880.

Conversation, as It Was by the Social Fireside, in the Time of the Tudors. 1880.

A Curious Experience. 1881.

The Prince and the Pauper: A Tale for Young People of All Ages. 1882.

The Stolen White Elephant, etc. 1882.

Life on the Mississippi. 1883.

Adventures of Huckleberry Finn (Tom Sawyer's Comrade). 1885.

Copy of a Letter Written in Answer to Inquiries Made by a Personal Friend. c. 1887.

A Connecticut Yankee in King Arthur's Court. 1889.

Facts for Mark Twain's Memory Builder. 1891.

The American Claimant. 1892.

Merry Tales. 1892.

The £1,000,000 Bank-Note and Other New Stories. 1893.

Pudd'nhead Wilson's Calendar for 1894. 1893.

Tom Sawyer Abroad. 1894.

The Tragedy of Pudd'nhead Wilson: A Tale. 1894.

Personal Recollections of Joan of Arc. 1896.

Tom Sawyer Abroad, Tom Sawyer, Detective, and Other Stories. 1896.

How to Tell a Story and Other Essays. 1897.

In Memoriam: Olivia Susan Clemens. 1897.

Following the Equator: A Journey around the World. 1897.

Writings (Autograph Edition). 1899–1900. 22 vols.

Writings (Author's National Edition). 1899–1910. 25 vols.

The Pains of Lowly Life. 1900.

The Man That Corrupted Hadleyburg and Other Stories and Essays. 1900.

A Salutation Speech from the Nineteenth Century to the Twentieth. 1900.

English as She Is Taught. 1900.

Edmund Burke on Croker and Tammany. 1901.

A Double Barrelled Detective Story. 1902.

Extract of a Letter to Frederick W. Peabody. c. 1902.

Extracts from Adam's Diary. 1904.

To Whom This Shall Come. 1904.

A Dog's Tale. 1904.

King Leopold's Soliloquy: A Defense of His Congo Rule. 1905.

Mark Twain on Vivisection. c. 1905.

Eve's Diary. 1906.

What Is Man? 1906.

The $30,000 Bequest and Other Stories. 1906.

Mark Twain on Simplified Spelling. 1906.

A Birthplace Worth Saving. 1906.

Christian Science, with Notes Containing Corrections to Date. 1907.

A Horse's Tale. 1907.

Is Shakespeare Dead? From My Autobiography. 1909.

Extract from Captain Stormfield's Visit to Heaven. 1909.

Speeches. Ed. F. A. Nott. 1910.

Queen Victoria's Jubilee. c. 1910.

The Suppressed Chapter of Life on the Mississippi. c. 1913.

The Mysterious Stranger: A Romance. 1916.

What Is Man? and Other Essays. 1917.

Letters. Ed. Albert Bigelow Paine. 1917. 2 vols.

The Mysterious Stranger and Other Stories. 1922.

Writings (Definitive Edition). 1922–25. 37 vols.

Speeches. Ed. Albert Bigelow Paine. 1923.

Europe and Elsewhere. Ed. Albert Bigelow Paine. 1923.

Autobiography. Ed. Albert Bigelow Paine. 1924. 2 vols.

Sketches of the Sixties (with Bret Harte). 1926.

The Quaker City Holy Land Excursion: An Unfinished Play. 1927.

The Suppressed Chapter of Following the Equator. 1928.

Notebook. Ed. Albert Bigelow Paine. 1935.

Letters from the Sandwich Islands. 1937.

The Washoe Giant in San Francisco: Being Heretofore Uncollected Sketches. Ed. Franklin Walker. 1938.

Letters from Honolulu Written for the Sacramento Union. 1939.

Travels with Mr. Brown: Being Heretofore Uncollected Sketches. Ed. Franklin Walker and Ezra Dane. 1940.

Mark Twain in Eruption: Hitherto Unpublished Pages about Men and Events. Ed. Bernard De Voto. 1940.

Republican Letters. Ed. Cyril Clemens. 1941.

Mark Twain, Business Man. Ed. Samuel Charles Webster. 1946.

The Portable Mark Twain. Ed. Bernard De Voto. 1946.

The Letters of Quintus Curtius Snodgrass. Ed. Ernest E. Leisy. 1946.

Mark Twain to Mrs. Fairbanks. Ed. Dixon Wecter. 1949.

Love Letters. Ed. Dixon Wecter. 1949.

Some Thoughts on the Science of Onanism. 1952.

Mark Twain to Uncle Remus 1881–1885. Ed. Thomas H. English. 1953.

Complete Short Stories. Ed. Charles Neider. 1957.

Mark Twain of the Enterprise: *Newspaper Articles and Other Documents 1862–1864.* Ed. Henry Nash Smith and Frederick Anderson. 1957.

Mark Twain, San Francisco Virginia City Territorial Enterprise *Correspondent: Selections from His Letters to the* Territorial Enterprise *1865–1866.* Ed. Henry Nash Smith and Frederick Anderson. 1957.

Traveling with the Innocents Abroad: Mark Twain's Original Reports from Europe and the Holy Land. Ed. Daniel Morley McKeithan. 1958.

Concerning Cats: Two Tales. 1959.

Mark Twain and the Government. Ed. Svend Peterson. 1960.

The Mark Twain–Howells Letters (with William Dean Howells). Ed. Henry Nash Smith, William B. Gibson, and Frederick Anderson. 1960. 2 vols.

Complete Humorous Sketches and Tales. Ed. Charles Neider. 1961.

Contributions to The Galaxy *1868–1871.* Ed. Bruce R. McElderry, Jr. 1961.

Life as I Find It: Essays, Sketches, and Other Material. Ed. Charles Neider. 1961.

Mark Twain's Letters to Mary. Ed. Lewis Leary. 1961.

The Pattern for Mark Twain's Roughing It: *Letters from Nevada by Samuel and Orion Clemens 1861–1862.* Ed. Franklin R. Rogers. 1961.

Ah Sin: A Dramatic Work (with Bret Harte). Ed. Frederick Anderson. 1961.

Letters from the Earth. Ed. Bernard De Voto. 1962.

Mark Twain on the Damned Human Race. Ed. Janet Smith. 1962.

Selected Shorter Writings. Ed. Walter Blair. 1962.

Complete Essays. Ed. Charles Neider. 1963.

Forgotten Writings. Ed. Henry Duskis. 1963.

Mark Twain's San Francisco. Ed. Bernard Taper. 1963.

Simon Wheeler, Detective. Ed. Franklin R. Rogers. 1963.

Complete Novels. Ed. Charles Neider. 1964. 2 vols.

Great Short Works. Ed. Justin Kaplan. 1967.

The Mark Twain Papers. Ed. Frederick Anderson et al. 1967– .

Clemens of the Call: *Mark Twain in San Francisco.* Ed. Edgar M. Branch. 1969.

Letters to the Rogers Family. Ed. Earl J. Dias. 1970.

Works. Ed. Frederick Anderson et al. 1972– .

Mark Twain Speaking. Ed. Paul Fatout. 1976.

The Comic Mark Twain Reader. Ed. Charles Neider. 1977.

The Devil's Race-Track: Mark Twain's Great Dark Writings. Ed. John S. Tuckey. 1980.

Selected Letters. Ed. Charles Neider. 1982.

Selected Writings of an American Skeptic. Ed. Victor Doyno. 1983.

Mark Twain's West: The Author's Memoirs about His Boyhood, Riverboats, and Western Adventures. Ed. Walter Blair. 1983.

The Hidden Mark Twain. Ed. Anne Ficklen. 1984.

The Science Fiction of Mark Twain. Ed. David Ketterer. 1984.

Plymouth Rock and the Pilgrims and Other Salutary Platform Opinions. Ed. Charles Neider. 1984.

Mark Twain at His Best. Ed. Charles Neider. 1986.

Mark Twain's Aquarium: The Samuel Clemens Angelfish Correspondence 1905–1910. Ed. John Cooley. 1991.

Works about
Mark Twain and
Adventures of Huckleberry Finn

Anderson, Frederick, ed. *Mark Twain: The Critical Heritage.* London: Routledge & Kegan Paul, 1971.

Auden, W. H. "Huck and Oliver." *Listener,* 1 October 1953, pp. 540–41.

Banta, Martha. "Rebirth or Revenge: The Endings of *Huckleberry Finn* and *The American." Modern Fiction Studies* 15 (1969–70): 191–207.

Bassett, John E. "Tom, Huck, and the Young Pilot: Twain's Quest for Authority." *Mississippi Quarterly* 39 (1985–86): 3–19.

Beaver, Harold. *Huckleberry Finn.* London: Allen & Unwin, 1987.

Bellamy, Gladys. *Mark Twain as a Literary Artist.* Norman: University of Oklahoma Press, 1950.

Blair, Walter. *Mark Twain and Huck Finn.* Berkeley: University of California Press, 1960.

———, ed. *Mark Twain's Hannibal, Huck, and Tom.* Berkeley: University of California Press, 1969.

Blakemore, Steven. "Huck Finn's Written World." *American Literary Realism* 21 (1988): 21–29.

Bloom, Harold, ed. *Huck Finn.* New York: Chelsea House, 1990.

———, ed. *Mark Twain's* Adventures of Huckleberry Finn. New York: Chelsea House, 1986.

Branch, Edgar. "The Two Providences: Thematic Form in *Huckleberry Finn." College English* 9 (1950): 188–95.

Budd, Louis J., ed. *New Essays on* Adventures of Huckleberry Finn. Cambridge: Cambridge University Press, 1985.

Burg, David F. "Another View of Huckleberry Finn." *Nineteenth-Century Fiction* 29 (1974): 299–319.

Camfield, Gregg. S*entimental Twain: Samuel Clemens in the Maze of Moral Philosophy*. Philadelphia: University of Pennsylvania Press, 1994.

Carkeet, David. "The Dialects in *Huckleberry Finn*." *American Literature* 51 (1979): 315–32.

Champion, Laurie, ed. *The Critical Response to Mark Twain's* Huckleberry Finn. Westport, CT: Greenwood Press, 1991.

Davis, Sara, and Philip Beidler, ed. *The Mythologizing of Mark Twain*. University: University of Alabama Press, 1984.

De Voto, Bernard. *Mark Twain's America*. Boston: Little, Brown, 1932.

Doyno, Victor A. *Writing Huck Finn: Mark Twain's Creative Process*. Philadelphia: University of Pennsylvania Press, 1991.

Egan, Michael. *Mark Twain's* Huckleberry Finn: *Race, Class, and Society*. London: Sussex University Press/Chatto & Windus, 1977.

Eliot, T. S. "Introduction" to *Adventures of Huckleberry Finn*. London: Cresset Press, 1950, pp. vii–xvi.

Emerson, Everett. T*he Authentic Mark Twain: A Literary Biography of Samuel L. Clemens*. Philadelphia: University of Pennsylvania Press, 1984.

Fetterley, Judith. "Disenchantment: Tom Sawyer in *Huckleberry Finn*." *PMLA* 87 (1972): 69–74.

Fiedler, Leslie A. "Come Back to the Raft Ag'in, Huck Honey!" *Partisan Review* 15 (1948): 664–71.

Fishkin, Shelley Fisher. *Was Huck Black? Mark Twain and African-American Voices*. New York: Oxford University Press, 1993.

Giddings, Robert, ed. *Mark Twain: A Sumptuous Variety*. London: Vision Press; New York: Barnes & Noble, 1985.

Gollin, Richard, and Gita Gollin. "*Huckleberry Finn* and the Time of the Evasion." *Modern Language Studies* 9 (1979): 5–15.

Harris, Susan K. *Mark Twain's Escape from Time: A Study of Patterns and Images.* Columbia: University of Missouri Press, 1982.

Haupt, Clyde V. Huckleberry Finn *on Film: Film and Television Adaptations of Mark Twain's Novel 1920–1993.* Jefferson, NC: McFarland, 1994.

Hill, Hamlin. *Mark Twain: God's Fool.* New York: Harper & Row, 1973.

Hoffman, Andrew Jay. *Twain's Heroes, Twain's Worlds: Mark Twain's* Adventures of Huckleberry Finn, A Connecticut Yankee in King Arthur's Court, *and* Pudd'nhead Wilson. Philadelphia: University of Pennsylvania Press, 1988.

Hoffman, Michael J. "Huck's Ironic Circle." *Georgia Review* 23 (1969): 307–22.

Holland, Laurence. "A 'Raft of Trouble': Word and Deed in *Huckleberry Finn.*" *Glyph* 5 (1979): 69–87.

Howells, W. D. *My Mark Twain: Reminiscences and Criticism.* New York: Harper & Brothers, 1910.

Inge, M. Thomas, ed. *Huck Finn among the Critics: A Centennial Selection.* Frederick, MD: University Publications of America, 1985.

Johnson, James L. *Mark Twain and the Limits of Power: Emerson's God in Ruins.* Knoxville: University of Tennessee Press, 1982.

Kaplan, Justin. *Born to Trouble: One Hundred Years of* Huckleberry Finn. Washington, DC: Library of Congress, 1985.

Kastely, James L. "The Ethics of Self-Interest: Narrative Logic in *Huckleberry Finn.*" *Nineteenth-Century Fiction* 40 (1986): 412–37.

Lauber, John. *The Many Inventions of Mark Twain.* New York: Hill & Wang, 1990.

MacKethan, Lucinda H. "Huckleberry Finn and the Slave Narratives: Lighting Out as Design." *Southern Review* 20 (1984): 247–64.

Mandia, Patricia M. *Comedic Pathos: Black Humor in Twain's Fiction.* Jefferson, NC: McFarland, 1991.

Opdahl, Keith M. "You'll Be Sorry When I'm Dead: Child Adult Relations in *Huck Finn.*" *Modern Fiction Studies* 25 (1979–80): 613–24.

Paine, Albert Bigelow. *Mark Twain: A Biography.* New York: Harper & Brothers, 1912. 4 vols.

Pettit, Arthur Gordon. *Mark Twain and the South.* Lexington: University Press of Kentucky, 1974.

Quirk, Tom. *Coming to Grips with* Huckleberry Finn: *Essays on a Book, a Boy, and a Man.* Columbia: University of Missouri Press, 1993.

Robinson, Forrest G. *In Bad Faith: The Dynamics of Deception in Mark Twain's America.* Cambridge, MA: Harvard University Press, 1986.

Rubin, Louis D., Jr. "Mark Twain's South: Tom and Huck." In *The American South: Portrait of a Culture,* ed. Louis D. Rubin, Jr. Baton Rouge: Louisiana State University Press, 1980, pp. 190–205.

Schacht, Paul. "The Lonesomeness of Huckleberry Finn." *American Literature* 53 (1981): 189–201.

Sewell, David R. *Mark Twain's Languages: Discourse, Dialogue, and Linguistic Variety.* Berkeley: University of California Press, 1987.

Skandera-Trombley, Laura E. *Mark Twain in the Company of Women.* Philadelphia: University of Pennsylvania Press, 1994.

Sloane, David E. E. *Mark Twain as a Literary Comedian.* Baton Rouge: Louisiana State University Press, 1979.

Smith, Henry Nash. *Mark Twain: The Development of a Writer.* Cambridge, MA: Harvard University Press, 1962.

Stahl, J. D. *Mark Twain, Culture and Gender: Envisioning America through Europe.* Athens: University of Georgia Press, 1994.

Steinbrink, Jeffrey. *Getting to Be Mark Twain.* Berkeley: University of California Press, 1991.

Stone, Albert E. *The Innocent Eye: Childhood in Mark Twain's Imagination.* New Haven: Yale University Press, 1961.

Stoneley, Peter. *Mark Twain and the Feminine Aesthetic.* Cambridge: Cambridge University Press, 1992.

Sundquist, Eric J., ed. *Mark Twain: A Collection of Critical Essays.* Englewood Cliffs, NJ: Prentice-Hall, 1994.

Towers, Tom H. "Love and Power in *Huckleberry Finn.*" *Tulane Studies in English* 23 (1978): 17–37.

Trachtenberg, Alan. "The Form of Freedom in *Huckleberry Finn.*" *Southern Review* 6 (1970): 954–71.

Vallin, Marlene Boyd. *Mark Twain: Protagonist for the Popular Culture.* Westport, CT: Greenwood Press, 1992.

Young, Philip. "*Huckleberry Finn:* The Little Lower Layer." In Young's *Three Bags Full: Essays in American Fiction.* New York: Harcourt Brace Jovanovich, 1972, pp. 136–53.

Index of
Themes and Ideas